The Glasgow Pascal Compiler
with vector extensions*

Paul Cockshott

June 27, 2011

*ISBN 978-1-4477-6156-3 ,

Contents

Introduction

Pascal[22] is an old programming language whose relative popularity has declined over the years, but like Fortran and C it lends itself to efficient code generation. Vector Pascal was first developed by Turner[36] and Formella[12]. It supports whole array operations in a manner that is similar to Fortran 90. This manual describes the Glasgow Pascal Compiler which supports vector extensions similar to those developed by Turner and Formella.

Modern processors have provision for parallelism in two ways:

1. The Single Instruction-stream Multiple Data-stream (SIMD) model in which a single instruction causes the same mathematical operation to be carried out on several operands, or pairs of operands at the same time. The level of parallelism supported ranges from 2 floating point operations at a time on the older AMD K6 architecture to 8 floating point operations at a time on the Intel AVX architecture.

2. The provision of multiple cores on one chip which execute parallel instructionsets. These may all run the same instructionset as on Intel processors, or run distinct instructionsets as on the IBM Cell chip.

Whilst processor architectures are moving towards greater levels of parallelism, the most widely used programming languages like C, Java and Delphi are structured around a model of computation in which operations take place on a single value at a time. This was appropriate when processors worked this way, but has become an impediment to programmers seeking to make use of the performance offered by multi-media instructionsets. The introduction of SIMD instruction sets[14][29] to Personal Computers potentially provided substantial performance increases, but the ability of most programmers to harness this performance was held back by two factors. The first was the limited availability of compilers that make effective use of these instructionsets in a machine independent manner. The second is the fact that most popular programming languages were designed on the word at a time model of the classic von Neumann computer.

The Glasgow Pascal Compiler aims to provide an efficient and concise notation for programmers using Multi-core and SIMD enhanced CPUs. In doing so it borrows concepts for expressing data parallelism that have a long history, dating back to Iverson's work on APL in the early '60s[18].

Define a vector of type T as having type $T[]$. Then if we have a binary operator $\omega : (T \otimes T) \rightarrow T$, in languages derived from APL we automatically have an operator $\omega : (T[] \otimes T[]) \rightarrow T[]$. Thus if x, y are arrays of integers $k = x + y$ is the array of integers where $k_i = x_i + y_i$.

The basic concept is simple, there are complications to do with the semantics of operations between arrays of different lengths and different dimensions, but

Iverson provides a consistent treatment of these. The most recent languages to be built round this model are J, an interpretive language[20][5][21], and F[28] a modernised Fortran. In principle though any language with array types can be extended in a similar way. Iverson's approach to data parallelism is machine independent. It can be implemented using scalar instructions or using the SIMD model. The only difference is speed.

Vector Pascal incorporates Iverson's approach to data parallelism. Its aim is to provide a notation that allows the natural and elegant expression of data parallel algorithms within a base language that is already familiar to a considerable body of programmers and combine this with modern compilation techniques.

By an elegant algorithm I mean one which is expressed as concisely as possible. Elegance is a goal that one approaches asymptotically, approaching but never attaining[7]. APL and J allow the construction of very elegant programs, but at a cost. An inevitable consequence of elegance is the loss of redundancy. APL programs are as concise, or even more concise than conventional mathematical notation[19] and use a special character-set. This makes them hard for the uninitiated to understand. J attempts to remedy this by restricting itself to the ASCII character-set, but still looks dauntingly unfamiliar to programmers brought up on more conventional languages. Both APL and J are interpretive which makes them ill suited to many of the applications for which SIMD speed is required. The aim of Vector Pascal is to provide the conceptual gains of Iverson's notation within a framework familiar to imperative programmers.

Pascal[22]was chosen as a base language over the alternatives of C and Java. C was rejected because notations like `x+y` for `x` and `y` declared as `int x[4], y[4]`, already have the meaning of adding the addresses of the arrays together. Java was rejected because of the difficulty of efficiently transmitting data parallel operations via its intermediate code to a just in time code generator.

Iverson's approach to data parallelism is machine independent. It can be implemented using scalar instructions or using the SIMD model. The only difference is speed. Vector Pascal incorporates Iverson's approach to data parallelism.

1 Elements of the language

1.1 Alphabet

The Vector Pascal compiler accepts files in the UTF-8 encoding of Unicode as source. Since ASCII is a subset of this, ASCII files are valid input.

Vector Pascal programs are made up of letter, digits and special symbols. The letters digits and special symbols are draw either from a base character set or from an extended character set. The base character set is drawn from ASCII and restricts the letters to be from the Latin alphabet. The extended character set allows letters from other alphabets.

The special symbols used in the base alphabet are shown in table1.1 .

1.1.1 Extended alphabet

The extended alphabet is described in Using Unicode with Vector Pascal.

1.2 Reserved words

The reserved words are

```
  ABS, ADDR, AND, ARRAY,
  BEGIN, BYTE2PIXEL,
  CASE, CAST, CDECL, CHR, CONST, COS,
   DIV, DO, DOWNTO,
  END, ELSE, EXIT, EXTERNAL,
  FALSE, FILE, FOR, FUNCTION,
  GOTO,
  IF, IMPLEMENTATION, IN, INTERFACE, IOTA,
  LABEL, LIBRARY, LN,
  MAX, MIN, MOD,
  NAME, NDX, NOT,
  OF, OR, ORD, OTHERWISE,
  PACKED, PERM, PIXEL2BYTE, POW, PRED,
PROCEDURE, PROGRAM, PROTECTED ,
  RDU, RECORD, REPEAT, ROUND,
  SET, SHL, SHR, SIN, SIZEOF, STRING, SQRT, SUCC,
  TAN, THEN, TO, TRANS, TRUE, TYPE,
  VAR,
  WITH, WHILE,  UNIT, UNTIL, USES
```

Reserved words may be written in either lower case or upper case letters, or any combination of the two.

Table 1.1: Special symbols

+	:	(
-	'	)
*	=	[
/	<>	]
:=	<	{
.	<=	}
,	>=	^
;	>	..
+:	@	*)
-:	$	(*
_	**	

1.3 Comments

The comment construct

{ < any sequence of characters not containing "}" > }

may be inserted between any two identifiers, special symbols, numbers or reserved words without altering the semantics or syntactic correctness of the program. The bracketing pair `(* *)` may substitute for `{ }`. Where a comment starts with `{` it continues until the next `}`. Where it starts with `(*` it must be terminated by `*)`[1].

1.4 Identifiers

Identifiers are used to name values, storage locations, programs, program modules, types, procedures and functions. An identifier starts with a letter followed by zero or more letters, digits or the special symbol `_`. Case is not significant in identifiers. ISO Pascal allows the Latin letters A-Z to be used in identifiers. Vector Pascal extends this by allowing symbols from the Greek, Cyrillic, Katakana and Hiragana, or CJK character sets

1.5 Literals

1.5.1 Integer numbers

Integer numbers are formed of a sequence of decimal digits, thus `1`, `23`, `9976` etc, or as hexadecimal numbers, or as numbers of any base between 2 and 36. A hexadecimal number takes the form of a $ followed by a sequence of hexadecimal digits thus `$01, $3ff, $5A`. The letters in a hexadecimal number may be upper or lower case and drawn from the range `a..f` or `A..F`.

[1]Note this differs from ISO Pascal which allows a comment starting with { to terminate with *) and vice versa.

Table 1.2: The hexadecimal digits of Vector Pascal.

Value	0	1	2	3	4	5	6	7	8	9	10	11	12	13	14	15
Notation 1	0	1	2	3	4	5	6	7	8	9	A	B	C	D	E	F
Notation 2	0	1	2	3	4	5	6	7	8	9	a	b	c	d	e	f

.

A based integer is written with the base first followed by a # character and then a sequence of letters or digits. Thus `2#1101` is a binary number `8#67` an octal number and `20#7i` a base 20 number.

The default precision for integers is 32 bits[2].

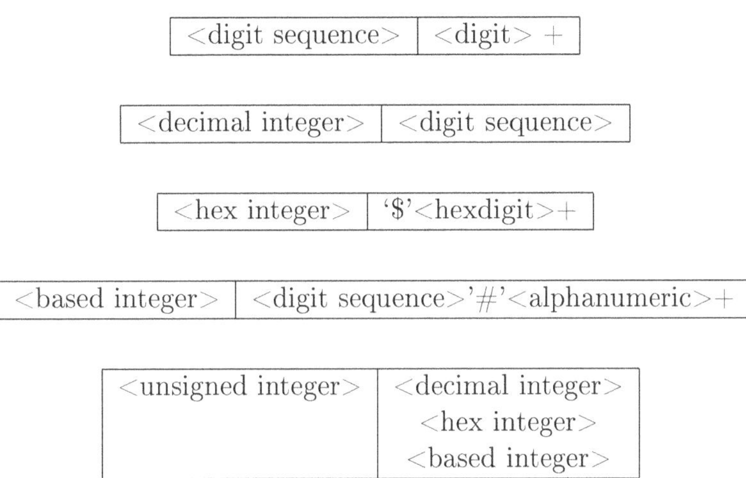

<digit sequence>	<digit> +

<decimal integer>	<digit sequence>

<hex integer>	'$'<hexdigit>+

<based integer>	<digit sequence>'#'<alphanumeric>+

<unsigned integer>	<decimal integer> <hex integer> <based integer>

1.5.2 Real numbers

Real numbers are supported in floating point notation, thus `14.7`, `9.99e5`, `38E3`, `3.6e-4` are all valid denotations for real numbers. The default precision for real numbers is also 32 bit, though intermediate calculations may use higher precision. The choice of 32 bits as the default precision is influenced by the fact that 32 bit floating point vector operations are well supported in multi-media instructions.

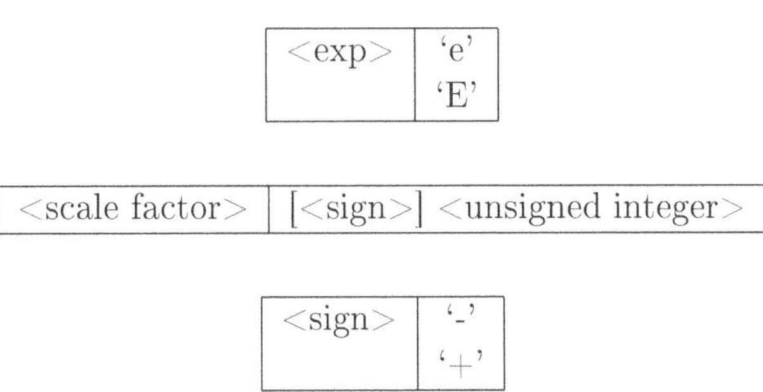

<exp>	'e' 'E'

<scale factor>	[<sign>] <unsigned integer>

<sign>	'-' '+'

[2]The notation used for grammar definition is a tabularised BNF . Each boxed table defines a production, with the production name in the left column. Each line in the right column is an alternative for the production. The metasymbol + indicates one or more repetitions of what immediately preceeds it. The Kleene star * is used for zero or more repetitions. Terminal symbols are in single quotes. Sequences in brackets [ ] are optional.

<unsigned real>	<decimal integer> '.' <digit sequence> <decimal integer>' .' <digit sequence> <exp><scale factor> <decimal integer><exp> <scale factor>

Fixed point numbers

In Vector Pascal pixels are represented as signed fixed point fractions in the range -1.0 to 1.0. Within this range, fixed point literals have the same syntactic form as real numbers.

1.5.3 Character strings

Sequences of characters enclosed by quotes are called literal strings. Literal strings consisting of a single character are constants of the standard type char. If the string is to contain a quote character this quote character must be written twice.

```
'A' 'x' 'hello' 'John''s house'
```

are all valid literal strings. The allowable characters in literal strings are any of the Unicode characters above u0020. The character strings must be input to the compiler in UTF-8 format.

2 Declarations

Vector Pascal is a language supporting nested declaration contexts. A declaration context is either a program context, and unit interface or implementation context, or a procedure or function context. A resolution context determines the meaning of an identifier. Within a resolution context, identifiers can be declared to stand for constants, types, variables, procedures or functions. When an identifier is used, the meaning taken on by the identifier is that given in the closest containing resolution context. Resolution contexts are any declaration context or a `with` statement context. The ordering of these contexts when resolving an identifier is:

1. The declaration context identified by any `with` statements which nest the current occurrence of the identifier. These `with` statement contexts are searched from the innermost to the outermost.
2. The declaration context of the currently nested procedure declarations. These procedure contexts are searched from the innermost to the outermost.
3. The declaration context of the current unit or program.
4. The interface declaration contexts of the units mentioned in the use list of the current unit or program. These contexts are searched from the rightmost unit mentioned in the use list to the leftmost identifier in the use list.
5. The interface declaration context of the System unit.
6. The pre-declared identifiers of the language.

2.1 Constants

A constant definition introduces an identifier as a synonym for a constant.

<constant declaration>	<identifier>=<expression>
	<identifier>':'<type>'='<typed constant>

Constants can be simple constants or typed constants. A simple constant must be a constant expression whose value is known at compile time. This restricts it to expressions for which all component identifiers are other constants, and for which the permitted operators are given in table2.1 . This restricts simple constants to be of scalar or string types.

Typed constants provide the program with initialised variables which may hold array types.

Table 2.1: The operators permitted in Vector Pascal constant expressions.

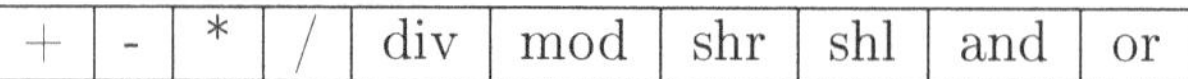

+	-	*	/	div	mod	shr	shl	and	or

<typed constant>	<expression> <array constant>

2.1.1 Array constants

Array constants are comma separated lists of constant expressions enclosed by brackets. Thus

```
tr:array[1..3] of real =(1.0,1.0,2.0);
```

is a valid array constant declaration, as is:

```
t2:array[1..2,1..3] of real=((1.0,2.0,4.0),(1.0,3.0,9.0));
```

The array constant must structurally match the type given to the identifier. That is to say it must match with respect to number of dimensions, length of each dimension, and type of the array elements.

<array constant>	'(' <typed constant> [,<typed constant>]* ')'

2.1.2 Pre-declared constants

`maxint` The largest supported integer value.

`pi` A real numbered approximation to π

`maxchar` The highest character in the character set.

`maxstring` The maximum number of characters allowed in a string.

`maxreal` The highest representable real.

`minreal` The smallest representable positive real number.

`epsreal` The smallest real number which when added to 1.0 yields a value distinguishable from 1.0.

`maxdouble` The highest representable double precision real number.

`mindouble` The smallest representable positive double precision real number.

`complexzero` A complex number with zero real and imaginary parts.

`complexone` A complex number with real part 1 and imaginary part 0.

2.2 Labels

Labels are written as digit sequences. Labels must be declared before they are used. They can be used to label the start of a statement and can be the destination of a `goto` statement. A `goto` statement must have as its destination a label declared within the current innermost declaration context. A statement can be prefixed by a label followed by a colon.

Example

```
label 99;
begin read(x); if x>9 goto 99; write(x*2);99:  end;
```

2.3 Types

A type declaration determines the set of values that expressions of this type may assume and associates with this set an identifier.

<type>	<simple type> <structured type> <pointer type>

<type definition>	<identifier>'='<type>

2.3.1 Simple types

Simple types are either scalar, standard, subrange or dimensioned types.

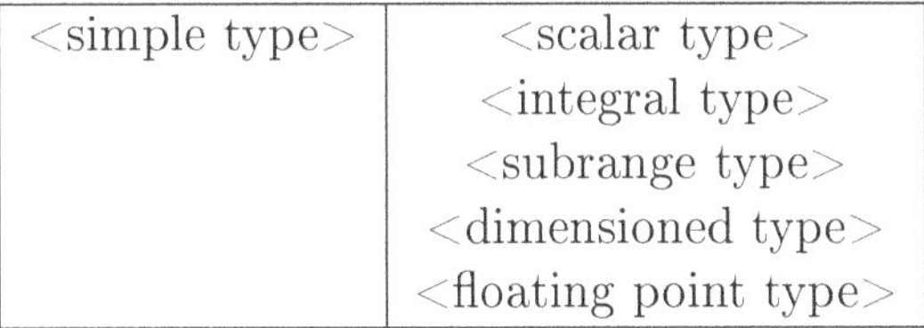

<simple type>	<scalar type> <integral type> <subrange type> <dimensioned type> <floating point type>

Scalar types

A scalar type defines an ordered set of identifier by listing these identifiers. The declaration takes the form of a comma separated list of identifiers enclosed by brackets. The identifiers in the list are declared simultaneously with the declared scalar type to be constants of this declared scalar type. Thus

```
colour = (red,green,blue);
day=(monday,tuesday,wednesday,thursday,
     friday,saturday,sunday);
```

are valid scalar type declarations.

Table 2.2: Categorisation of the standard types.

type	category
real	floating point
double	floating point
byte	integral
pixel	fixed point
shortint	integral
word	integral
integer	integral
cardinal	integral
boolean	scalar
char	scalar

Standard types

The following types are provided as standard in Vector Pascal:

`integer` The numbers are in the range -maxint to +maxint.

`real` These are a subset of the reals constrained by the IEEE 32 bit floating point format.

`double` These are a subset of the real numbers constrained by the IEEE 64 bit floating point format.

`pixel` These are represented as fixed point binary fractions in the range -1.0 to 1.0.

`boolean` These take on the values `(false,true)` which are ordered such that `true>false`.

`char` These include the characters from `chr(0)` to `charmax`. All the allowed characters for string literals are in the type char, but the character-set may include other characters whose printable form is country specific.

`pchar` Defined as `^char`.

`byte` These take on the positive integers between 0 and 255.

`shortint` These take on the signed values between -128 and 127.

`word` These take on the positive integers from 0 to 65535.

`cardinal` These take on the positive integers form 0 to 4292967295, i.e., the most that can be represented in a 32 bit unsigned number.

`longint` A 32 bit integer, retained for compatibility with Turbo Pascal.

`int64` A 64 bit integer.

`complex` A complex number with the real and imaginary parts held to 32 bit precision.

Subrange types

A type may be declared as a subrange of another scalar or integer type by indicating the largest and smallest value in the subrange. These values must be constants known at compile time.

<subrange type>	<constant> '..' <constant>

Examples: 1..10, 'a'..'f', monday..thursday.

Pixels

The *conceptual model* of pixels in Vector Pascal is that they are real numbers in the range $-1.0..1.0$. As a signed representation it lends itself to subtraction. As an unbiased representation, it makes the adjustment of contrast easier. For example, one can reduce contrast 50% simply by multiplying an image by 0.5 [1]. Assignment to pixel variables in Vector Pascal is defined to be saturating - real numbers outside the range $-1..1$ are clipped to it. The multiplications involved in convolution operations fall naturally into place.

The *implementation model* of pixels used in Vector Pascal is of 8 bit signed integers treated as fixed point binary fractions. All the conversions necessary to preserve the monotonicity of addition, the range of multiplication etc, are delegated to the code generator which, where possible, will implement the semantics using efficient, saturated multi-media arithmetic instructions.

Dimensioned types

These provide a means by which floating point types can be specialised to represent dimensioned numbers as is required in physics calculations. For example:

```
kms =(mass,distance,time);
meter=real of distance;
kilo=real of mass;
second=real of time;
newton=real of mass * distance * time POW -2;
meterpersecond = real of distance *time POW -1;
```

The grammar is given by:

<dimensioned type>	<real type> <dimension >['*' <dimension>]*

<real type>	'real' 'double'

<dimension>	<identifier> ['POW' [<sign>] <unsigned integer>]

[1] When pixels are represented as integers in the range 0..255, a 50% contrast reduction has to be expressed as $((p - 128) \div 2) + 128$.

The identifier must be a member of a scalar type, and that scalar type is then referred to as the basis space of the dimensioned type. The identifiers of the basis space are referred to as the dimensions of the dimensioned type. Associated with each dimension of a dimensioned type there is an integer number referred to as the power of that dimension. This is either introduced explicitly at type declaration time, or determined implicitly for the dimensional type of expressions.

A value of a dimensioned type is a dimensioned value. Let $\log_d t$ of a dimensioned type t be the power to which the dimension d of type t is raised. Thus for t =newton in the example above, and d =time, $\log_d t = -2$

If x and y are values of dimensioned types $t_x$and $t_y$respectively, then the following operators are only permissible if $t_x = t_y$

+	-	<	>	<>	=	<=	>=

For + and -, the dimensional type of the result is the same as that of the arguments. The operations

are permitted if the types $t_x$and t_y share the same basis space, or if the basis space of one of the types is a subrange of the basis space of the other.

The operation `POW` is permitted between dimensioned types and integers.

Dimension deduction rules

1. If $x = y * z$ for $x : t_1, y : t_2, z : t_3$ with basis space B then

$$\forall_{d \in B} \log_d t_1 = \log_d t_2 + \log_d t_3$$

2. If $x = y/z$ for $x : t_1, y : t_2, z : t_3$ with basis space B then

$$\forall_{d \in B} \log_d t_1 = \log_d t_2 - \log_d t_3$$

3. If $x = y$ `POW` z for $x : t_1, y : t_2, z : integer$ with basis space for t_2, B then

$$\forall_{d \in B} \log_d t_1 = \log_d t_2 \times z$$

.

2.3.2 Structured types

Static Array types

An array type is a structure consisting of a fixed number of elements all of which are the same type. The type of the elements is referred to as the element type. The elements of an array value are indicated by bracketed indexing expressions. The definition of an array type simultaneously defines the permitted type of indexing expression and the element type.

The index type of a static array must be a scalar or subrange type. This implies that the bounds of a static array are known at compile time.

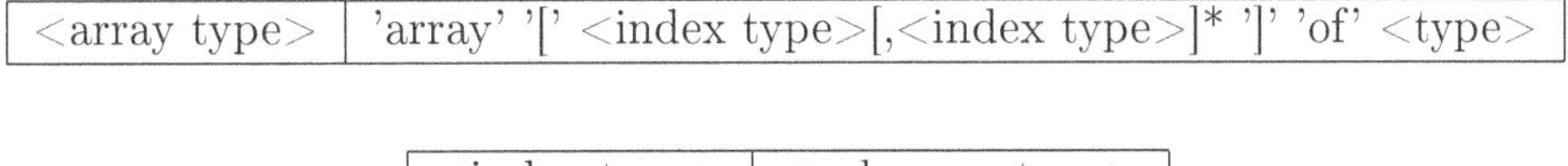

<array type>	'array' '[' <index type>[,<index type>]* ']' 'of' <type>

<index type>	<subrange type> <scalar type> <integral type>

Examples

```
array[colour] of boolean;
array[1..100] of integer;
array[1..2,4..6] of byte;
array[1..2] of array[4..6] of byte;
```

The notation [*b*,*c*] in an array declaration is shorthand for the notation [*b*] `of array` [*c*]. The number of dimensions of an array type is referred to as its rank. Scalar types have rank 0.

String types

A string type denotes the set of all sequences of characters up to some finite length and must have the syntactic form:

<string-type>	'string[' <integer constant>']' 'string' 'string(' <ingeger constant>')'

the integer constant indicates the maximum number of characters that may be held in the string type. The maximum number of characters that can be held in any string is indicated by the pre-declared constant `maxstring`. The type `string` is shorthand for `string[maxstring]`.

Record types

A record type defines a set of similar data structures. Each member of this set, a record instance, is a Cartesian product of number of components or *fields* specified in the record type definition. Each field has an identifier and a type. The scope of these identifiers is the record itself.

A record type may have as a final component a *variant part*. The variant part, if a variant part exists, is a union of several variants, each of which may itself be a Cartesian product of a set of fields. If a variant part exists there may be a tag field whose value indicates which variant is assumed by the record instance.

All field identifiers even if they occur within different variant parts, must be unique within the record type.

<record type>	'record' <field list> 'end'

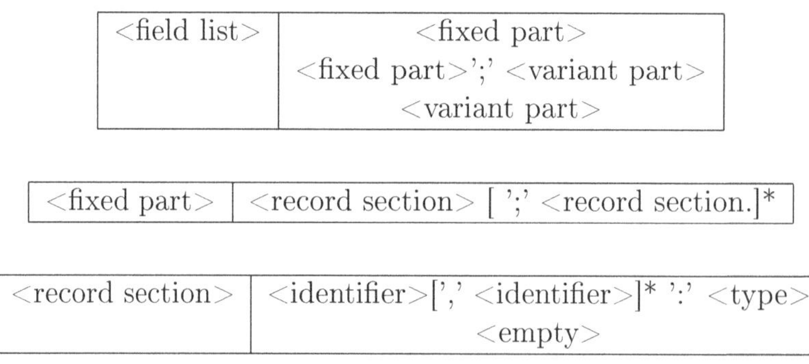

<field list>	<fixed part> <fixed part>';' <variant part> <variant part>

<fixed part>	<record section> [';' <record section.]*

<record section>	<identifier>[',' <identifier>]* ':' <type> <empty>

<variant part>	'case' [<tag field> ':'] <type identifier> 'of'<variant>[';' <variant>]*

<variant>	<constant> [',' <constant>]*':' '(' <field list> ')' <empty>

Set types

A set type defines the range of values which is the power-set of its base type. The base type must be an ordered type, that is a type on which the operations $<$, $=$ and $>$ are defined[2]. Thus sets may be declared whose base types are characters, numbers, ordinals, or strings. Any user defined type on which the comparison operators have been defined can also be the base type of a set.

<set type>	'set' 'of' <base type>

2.3.3 Dynamic types

Variables declared within the program are accessed by their identifier. These variables exist throughout the existence of the scope within which they are declared, be this unit, program or procedure. These variables are assigned storage locations whose addresses, either absolute or relative to some register, can be determined at compile time. Such locations a referred to as static[3]. Storage locations may also be allocated dynamically. Given a type `t`, the type of a pointer to an instance of type `t` is `^t`.

A pointer of type `^t` can be initialised to point to a new store location of type t by use of the built in procedure `new`. Thus if `p:^t`,

```
new(p);
```

[2]ISO Pascal requires the base type to be a scalar type, a character type, integer type or a subrange thereof. When the base type is one of these, Vector Pascal implements the set using bitmaps. When the type is other than these, balanced binary trees are used. It is strongly recomended that use be made of Boehm garbage collector (see section 5.2.2) if non-bitmapped sets are used in a program.

[3]The Pascal concept of static variables should not be equated with the notion of static variables in some other languages such as C or Java. In Pascal a variable is considered static if its offset either relative to the stack base or relative to the start of the global segment can be determined at compile/link time. In C a variable is static only if its location relative to the start of the global segment is known at compile time.

causes `p` to point at a store location of type `t`.

Pointers to dynamic arrays

The types pointed to by pointer types can be any of the types mentioned so far, that is to say, any of the types allowed for static variables. In addition however, pointer types can be declared to point at dynamic arrays. A dynamic array is an array whose bounds are determined at run time.

Pascal 90[16] introduced the notion of schematic or parameterised types as a means of creating dynamic arrays. Thus where `r` is some integral or ordinal type one can write

```
type z(a,b:r)=array[a..b] of t;
```

If `p:^z`, then

```
new(p,n,m)
```

where `n,m:r` initialises `p` to point to an array of bounds `n..m`. The bounds of the array can then be accessed as `p^.a, p^.b`. In this case `a, b` are the formal parameters of the array type. Vector Pascal currently only allows parameterised types to be allocated on the heap via `new`. The extended form of the procedure `new` must be passed an actual parameter for each formal parameter in the array type.

Dynamic arrays

Vector Pascal also allows the use of Delphi style declarations for dynamic arrays. Thus one can declare:

```
type vector = array of real;
     matrix = array of array of real;
```

The size of such arrays has to be explicitly initialised at runtime by a call to the library procedure `setlength`. Thus one might have:

```
function readtotal:real;
var len:integer;
    v:vector;
begin
 readln(len);
 setlength(v,len);
 readln(v);
 readtotal := \+ v;
end;
```

The function `readtotal` reads the number of elements in a vector from the standard input. It then calls `setlength` to initialise the vector length. Next it reads in the vector and computes its total using the reduction operator `\+`.

In the example, the variable `v` denotes an array of reals not a pointer to an array of reals. However, since the array size is not known at compile time `setlength` will allocate space for the array on the heap not in the local stack frame. The use of `setlength` is thus restricted to programs which have been

compiled with the garbage collection flag enabled (see section 5.2.2). The procedure `setlength` must be passed a parameter for each dimension of the dynamic array. The bounds of the array `a` formed by
`setlength(a,i,j,k)`
would then be `0..i-1, 0..j-1, 0..k-1.`

Low and High

The build in functions `low` and `high` return the lower and upper bounds of an array respectively. They work with both static and dynamic arrays. Consider the following examples.

```
program arrays;
type  z(a,b:integer)=array[a..b] of real;
      vec = array of real;
      line= array [1..80] of char;
      matrix = array of array of real;
var i:^z; v:vec; l:line; m:matrix;
begin
 setlength(v,10);setlength(m,5,4);
 new(i,11,13);
 writeln(low(v), high(v));
 writeln(low(m), high(m));
 writeln(low(m[0]),high(m[0]));
 writeln(low(l),high(l));
 writeln(low(i^),high(i^));
end.
```

would print

```
          0          9
          0          4
          0          3
          1         80
         11         13
```

2.4 File types

A type may be declared to be a file of a type. This form of definition is kept only for backward compatibility. All file types are treated as being equivalent. A file type corresponds to a handle to an operating system file. A file variable must be associated with the operating system file by using the procedures `assign, rewrite, append`, and `reset` provided by the system unit. A pre-declared file type `text` exists.

Text files are assumed to be in Unicode UTF-8 format. Conversions are performed between the internal representation of characters and UTF-8 on input/output from/to a text file.

2.5 Variables

Variable declarations consist of a list of identifiers denoting the new variables, followed by their types.

<variable declaration>	<identifier> [',' <identifier>]* ':' <type><extmod>

Variables are abstractions over values. They can be either simple identifiers, components or ranges of components of arrays, fields of records or referenced dynamic variables.

<variable>	<identifier>
	<indexed variable>
	<indexed range>
	<field designator>
	<referenced variable>

Examples

```
x,y:real;
i:integer;
point:^real;
dataset:array[1..n]of integer;
twoDdata:array[1..n,4..7] of real;
```

2.5.1 External Variables

A variable may be declared to be external by appending the external modifier.

<extmod>	';' 'external' 'name' <stringlit>

This indicates that the variable is declared in a non Vector Pascal external library. The name by which the variable is known in the external library is specified in a string literal.

Example

```
count:integer; external name '_count';
```

2.5.2 Entire Variables

An entire variable is denoted by its identifier. Examples `x,y,point`,

2.5.3 Indexed Variables

A component of an n dimensional array variable is denoted by the variable followed by n index expressions in brackets.

<indexed variable>	<variable>'[' <expression>[','<expression>]* ']'

The type of the indexing expression must conform to the index type of the array variable. The type of the indexed variable is the component type of the array.

Examples

`twoDdata[2,6]`
`dataset[i]`
Given the declaration
`a=array[p] of q`
then the elements of arrays of type `a`, will have type `q` and will be identified by indices of type `p` thus:
`b[i]`
where `i:p`, `b:a`.
Given the declaration
`z = string[x]`
for some integer x ≤`maxstring`, then the characters within strings of type `z` will be identified by indices in the range `1..x`, thus:
`y[j]`
where `y:z`, `j:1..x`.

Indexed Ranges

A range of components of an array variable are denoted by the variable followed by a range expression in brackets.

<indexed range>	<variable> '[' <range expression>[',' <range expression>]* ']'

<range expression>	<expression> '..' <expression>

The expressions within the range expression must conform to the index type of the array variable. The type of a range expression `a[i..j]` where `a: array[p..q] of t` is `array[0..j-i] of t`.

Examples:

```
dataset[i..i+2]:=blank;
twoDdata[2..3,5..6]:=twoDdata[4..5,11..12]*0.5;
```

Subranges may be passed in as actual parameters to procedures whose corresponding formal parameters are declared as variables of a schematic type. Hence given the following declarations:

```
type image(miny,maxy,minx,maxx:integer)=array[miny..maxy,minx..maxx]
of byte;
procedure invert(var im:image);begin im:=255-im; end;
var screen:array[0..319,0..199] of byte;
```

then the following statement would be valid:

```
invert(screen[40..60,20..30]);
```

Indexing arrays with arrays

If an array variable occurs on the right hand side of an assignment statement, there is a further form of indexing possible. An array may be indexed by another array. If `x:array[t0] of t1` and `y:array[t1] of t2`, then `y[x]` denotes the virtual array of type `array[t0] of t2` such that `y[x][i]=y[x[i]]`. This construct is useful for performing permutations. To fully understand the following example refer to sections 3.1.3,3.2.1.

Example Given the declarations

```
const perms:array[0..3] of integer=(3,1,2,0);
var ma,m0:array[0..3] of integer;
```

then the statements

```
m0:= (iota 0)+1;
write('m0=');for j:=0 to 3 do write(m0[j]);writeln;
ma:=m0[perms];
write('perms=');for j:=0 to 3 do write(perms[j]);writeln;
writeln('ma:=m0[perms]');for j:=0 to 3 do write(ma[j]);writeln;
```

would produce the output

```
m0= 1 2 3 4
perms=  3 1 2 0
ma:=m0[perms]
4 2 3 1
```

This basic method can also be applied to multi-dimensional array. Consider the following example of an image warp:

```
type pos   = 0..255;
     image      = array[pos,pos] of pixel;
     warper     = array[pos,pos,0..1] of pos;
var  im1 ,im2 :image;
     warp     :warper;
begin
    ....
    getbackwardswarp(warp);
    im2 := im1 [ warp ];
    ....
```

The procedure `getbackwardswarp` determines for each pixel position `x, y` in an image the position in the source image from which it is to be obtained. After the assignment we have the postcondition

$$\mathtt{im2}[\mathtt{x},\mathtt{y}] = \mathtt{im1}[\mathtt{warp}[\mathtt{x},\mathtt{y},0],\mathtt{warp}[\mathtt{x},\mathtt{y},1]]\forall \mathtt{x},\mathtt{y} \in \mathtt{pos}$$

2.5.4 Field Designators

A component of an instance of a record type, or the parameters of an instance of a schematic type are denoted by the record or schematic type instance followed by the field or parameter name.

<field designator>	<variable>'.'<identifier>

2.5.5 Referenced Variables

If `p:^t`, then `p^` denotes the dynamic variable of type `t` referenced by `p`.

<referenced variable>	<variable> '^'

2.6 Procedures and Functions

Procedure and function declarations allow algorithms to be identified by name and have arguments associated with them so that they may be invoked by procedure statements or function calls.

<procedure declaration>	<procedure heading>';'[<proc tail>]
<proc tail>	'forward' 'external' ['name' <string>] <block>
<paramlist>	'('<formal parameter sec>[';'<formal parameter sec>]*')'
<procedure heading>	'procedure' <identifier> [<paramlist>] 'function'<identifier> [<paramlist>]':'<type>
<formal parameter sec>	['var']<identifier>[','<identifier>]':'<type> <procedure heading>
<procedure type>	'procedure' [<paramlist>] 'function' [<paramlist>]':'<type>

The parameters declared in the procedure heading are local to the scope of the procedure. The parameters in the procedure heading are termed formal parameters. If the identifiers in a formal parameter section are preceded by the word `var`, then the formal parameters are termed variable parameters. The block[4] of a procedure or function constitutes a scope local to its executable compound statement. Within a function declaration there must be at least one statement assigning a value to the function identifier. This assignment determines the result of a function, but assignment to this identifier does not cause an immediate return from the function.

Function return values can be scalars, pointers, records, strings, static arrays or sets. Arrays whose size is determined at run time may not be returned from a function.

Where a procedure is declared as forward it must be followed by a full definition of procedure lower in the current scope.

The external declaration form allows calls to be made to libraries written in other languages.

Examples The function sba is the mirror image of the abs function.

```
function sba(i:integer):integer;
begin if i>o then sba:=-i else sba:=i end;
type stack:array[0..100] of integer;
procedure push(var s:stack;i:integer);
begin s[s[0]]:=i;s[0]:=s[0]+1; end;
```

```
procedure append(var f:fileptr);external;
procedure close (var f:fileptr); external name 'pasclose';
```

[4] see section 4.

2.6.1 Procedural Parameters to Procedures

A procedure may have parameters that are themselves procedures as shown in the following example.

```
program CONF103(output);
var
   i : integer;
procedure alsoconforms(x : integer);
begin
  writeln(' PASS...6.6.3.1-4 (CONF103)')
end;
procedure conforms(procedure alsoconforms(x : integer));
   var x : boolean;
begin
   x:=true;
   alsoconforms(1)
end;
begin
   i:=2;
   conforms(alsoconforms)
end.
```

2.6.2 Procedure types

Procedural types may be declared. This in turn allows procedure variables. These store the address of a procedure or function and can be assigned to using the address operator @.

Example

```
program procvar;
type t=procedure (x:integer);
var v:t;
    procedure f(a:integer);begin writeln(a);end;
begin
        v:= @f;
        v(3);
end.
```

3 Algorithms

3.1 Expressions

An expression is a rule for computing a value by the application of operators and functions to other values. These operators can be *monadic* - taking a single argument, or *dyadic* - taking two arguments.

3.1.1 Mixed type expressions

The arithmetic operators are defined over the base types integer and real. If a dyadic operator that can take either real or integer arguments is applied to arguments one of which is an integer and the other a real, the integer argument is first implicitly converted to a real before the operator is applied. Similarly, if a dyadic operator is applied to two integral numbers of different precision, the number of lower precision is initially converted to the higher precisions, and the result is of the higher precision. Higher precision of types t,u is defined such that the type with the greater precision is the one which can represent the largest range of numbers. Hence reals are taken to be higher precision than longints even though the number of significant bits in a real may be less than in a longint.

When performing mixed type arithmetic between pixels and another numeric data type, the values of both types are converted to reals before the arithmetic is performed. If the result of such a mixed type expression is subsequently assigned to a pixel variable, all values greater than 1.0 are mapped to 1.0 and all values below -1.0 are mapped to -1.0.

3.1.2 Primary expressions

<primary expression>	'(' <expression> ')'
	<literal string>
	'true'
	'false'
	<unsigned integer>
	<unsigned real>
	<variable>
	<constant id>
	<function call>
	<set construction>

The most primitive expressions are instances of the literals defined in the language: literal strings, boolean literals, literal reals and literal integers. 'Salerno', `true`, 12, \$ea8f, 1.2e9 are all primary expressions. The next level of abstraction is provided by symbolic identifiers for values. `X`, `left`, `a.max`, `p^.next`, `z[1]`, `image[4..200,100..150]` are all primary expressions provided that the identifiers have been declared as variables or constants.

An expression surrounded by brackets `( )` is also a primary expression. Thus if e is an expression so is `(` e `)`.

<function call>	<function id> ['(' <expression> [,<expression>]* ')']

<element>	<expression> <range expression>

Let e be an expression of type t_1 and if `f` is an identifier of type `function(`t_1 `)`:t_2, then `f(` e `)` is a primary expression of type t_2. A function which takes no parameters is invoked without following its identifier by brackets. It will be an error if any of the actual parameters supplied to a function are incompatible with the formal parameters declared for the function.

<set construction>	'[' [<element>[,<element>]*] ']'

Finally a primary expression may be a set construction. A set construction is written as a sequence of zero or more elements enclosed in brackets `[ ]` and separated by commas. The elements themselves are either expressions evaluating to single values or range expressions denoting a sequence of consecutive values. The type of a set construction is deduced by the compiler from the context in which it occurs. A set construction occurring on the right hand side of an assignment inherits the type of the variable to which it is being assigned. The following are all valid set constructions:

`[], [1..9], [z..j,9], [a,b,c,]`

`[]` denotes the empty set.

3.1.3 Unary expressions

A unary expression is formed by applying a unary operator to another unary or primary expression. The unary operators supported are `+, -, *, /, div, mod, and, or, not, round, sqrt, sin, cos, tan, abs, ln, ord, chr, byte2pixel, pixel2byte, succ, pred, iota, trans, addr` and `@`.

Thus the following are valid unary expressions: `-1`, `+b`, `not true`, `sqrt abs x`, `sin theta`. In standard Pascal some of these operators are treated as functions,. Syntactically this means that their arguments must be enclosed in brackets, as in `sin(theta)`. This usage remains syntactically correct in Vector Pascal.

The dyadic operators `+, -, *, /, div, mod , and or` are all extended to unary context by the insertion of an implicit value under the operation. Thus just as `-a = 0-a` so too `/2 = 1/2`. For sets the notation `-s` means the complement of the set `s`. The implicit value inserted are given below.

type	operators	`implicit value`
`number`	`+,-`	0
string	`+`	''
set	`+`	empty set
number	`*,/ ,div,mod`	1
number	`max`	lowest representable number of the type
number	`min`	highest representable number of the type
boolean	`and`	true
boolean	`or`	false

A unary operator can be applied to an array argument and returns an array result. Similarly any user declared function over a scalar type can be applied to an array type and return an array. If `f` is a function or unary operator mapping from type `r` to type `t` then if `x` is an array of `r,` and `a` an array of `t`, then `a:=f(x)` assigns an array of `t` such that `a[i]=f(x[i])`

<unary expression>	<unaryop> <unary expression> 'sizeof' '(' <type> ')' <operator reduction> <primary expression>
	'if'<expression> 'then' <expression> 'else' <expression>

sizeof

The construct `sizeof(` *t* `)` where *t* is a type, returns the number of bytes occupied by an instance of the type.

iota

The operator iota i returns the ith current implicit index[1].

Examples Thus given the definitions

```
var v1:array[1..3]of integer;
v2:array[0..4] of integer;
```

then the program fragment

```
v1:=iota 0;
v2:=iota 0 *2;

for i:=1 to 3 do write( v1[i]); writeln;
writeln('v2');
for i:=0 to 4 do write( v2[i]); writeln;
```

would produce the output

```
v1
1 2 3
v2
```

[1]See section 3.2.1.

Table 3.1: Unary operators

lhs	rhs	meaning
<unaryop>	'+'	+x = 0+x identity operator
	'-'	-x = 0-x,
		note: this is defined on integer, real and complex
	'*', '×'	*x=1*x identity operator
	'/'	/x=1.0/x
		note: this is defined on integer, real and complex
	'div', '÷'	div x =1 div x
	'mod'	mod x = 1 mod x
	'and'	and x = true and x
	'or'	or x = false or x
	'not', '¬'	complements booleans
	'round'	rounds a real to the closest integer
	'sqrt', '√'	returns square root as a real number.
	'sin'	sine of its argument. Argument in radians. Result is real.
	'cos'	cosine of its argument. Argument in radians. Result is real.
	'tan'	tangent of its argument. Argument in radians. Result is real.
	'abs'	if x<0 then abs x = -x else abs x= x
	'ln'	$\log_e$ of its argument. Result is real.
	'ord'	argument scalar type, returns ordinal
		number of the argument.
	'chr'	converts an integer into a character.
	'succ'	argument scalar type,
		returns the next scalar in the type.
	'pred'	argument scalar type,
		returns the previous scalar in the type.
	'iota', 'ι'	iota i returns the ith current index
	'trans'	transposes a matrix or vector
	'pixel2byte'	convert pixel in range -1.0..1.0 to byte in range 0..255
	'byte2pixel'	convert a byte in range 0..255 to a pixel in
		the range -1.0..1.0
	'@','addr'	Given a variable, this returns an
		untyped pointer to the variable.

```
0 2 4 6 8
```

whilst given the definitions

```
m1:array[1..3,0..4] of integer;m2:array[0..4,1..3]of integer;
```

then the program fragment

```
m2:= iota 0 +2*iota 1;
writeln('m2:= iota 0 +2*iota 1 ');
for i:=0 to 4 do begin for j:=1 to 3 do write(m2[i,j]); writeln; end;
```

would produce the output

```
m2:= iota 0 +2*iota 1
2 4 6
3 5 7
4 6 8
5 7 9
6 8 10
```

The argument to `iota` must be an integer known at compile time within the range of implicit indices in the current context. The reserved word `ndx` is a synonym for `iota`.

perm A generalised permutation of the implicit indices is performed using the syntactic form:

perm[*index-sel[,index-sel]*]expression*

The *index-sels* are integers known at compile time which specify a permutation on the implicit indices. Thus in e evaluated in context perm[i, j, k]e, then:

iota 0 = iota i, iota 1= iota j, iota 2= iota k

This is particularly useful in converting between different image formats. Hardware frame buffers typically represent images with the pixels in the red, green, blue, and alpha channels adjacent in memory. For image processing it is convenient to hold them in distinct planes. The `perm` operator provides a concise notation for translation between these formats:

```
type rowindex=0..479;
     colindex=0..639;
var channel=red..alpha;
    screen:array[rowindex,colindex,channel] of pixel;
    img:array[channel,colindex,rowindex] of pixel;
...
screen:=perm[2,0,1]img;
```

`trans` and `diag` provide shorthand notions for expressions in terms of `perm`. Thus in an assignment context of rank 2, `trans = perm[1,0]` and `diag = perm[0,0]`.

trans

The operator trans transposes a vector or matrix. It achieves this by cyclic rotation of the implicit indices. Thus if `trans` e is evaluated in a context with implicit indices

`iota` 0.. `iota` n

then the expression e is evaluated in a context with implicit indices

`iota'`0.. `iota'`n

where

`iota'`x = `iota` ($(x+1)$`mod` $n+1$)

It should be noted that transposition is generalised to arrays of rank greater than 2.

Examples Given the definitions used above in section 3.1.3, the program fragment:

```
m1:= (trans v1)*v2;
writeln('(trans v1)*v2');
for i:=1 to 3 do begin for j:=0 to 4 do write(m1[i,j]); writeln; end;

m2 := trans m1;
writeln('transpose 1..3,0..4 matrix');
for i:=0 to 4 do begin for j:=1 to 3 do write(m2[i,j]); writeln; end;
```

will produce the output:

```
(trans v1)*v2
0  2  4  6  8
0  4  8 12 16
0  6 12 18 24
transpose 1..3,0..4 matrix
0  0  0
2  4  6
4  8 12
6 12 18
8 16 24
```

3.1.4 Operator Reduction

Any dyadic operator can be converted to a monadic reduction operator by the functional $\backslash$. Thus if `a` is an array, `\+a` denotes the sum over the array. More generally $\backslash\Phi x$ for some dyadic operator Φ means $x_0\Phi(x_1\Phi..(x_n\Phi\iota))$ where ι is the implicit value given the operator and the type. Thus we can write `\+` for summation, `\*` for nary product etc. The dot product of two vectors can thus be written as

```
x:= \+ y*x;
```

instead of

```
x:=0;
```

```
for i:=0 to n do x:= x+ y[i]*z[i];
```

A reduction operation takes an argument of rank r and returns an argument of rank r-1 except in the case where its argument is of rank 0, in which case it acts as the identity operation. Reduction is always performed along the last array dimension of its argument.

The operations of summation and product can be be written eithter as the two functional forms \ + and \ * or as the prefix operators $\sum$ (Unicode 2211) and $\prod$ (Unicode 220f).

<operator reduction>	'\'<dyadic op> <multiplicative expression> '$\sum$' <mutliplicative expression> '$\prod$' < multiplicative expression>

<dyadic op>	<expop> <multop> <addop>

The reserved word **rdu** is available as a lexical alternative to \, so \+ is equivalent to `rdu+`.

3.1.5 Complex conversion

Complex numbers can be produced from reals using the function `cmplx`. `cmplx(`*re,im*`)` is the complex number with real part *re*, and imaginaray part *im*.

The real and imaginary parts of a complex number can be obtained by the functions `re` and `im`. `re`(c) is the real part of the complex number c. `im`(c) is the imaginary part of the complex number c.

3.1.6 Conditional expressions

The conditional expression allows two different values to be returned depenent upon a boolean expression.

```
var a:array[0..63] of real;
...

a:=if a>0 then a else -a;

...
```

The `if` expression can be compiled in two ways:

1. Where the two arms of the if expression are parallelisable, the condition and both arms are evaluated and then merged under a boolean mask. Thus, the above assignment would be equivalent to:

   ```
   a:= (a and (a>0))or(not (a>0) and -a);
   ```

were the above legal Pascal[2].

2. If the code is not paralleliseable it is translated as equivalent to a standard if statement. Thus, the previous example would be equivalent to:

   `for i:=0 to 63 do if a[i]>0 then a[i]:=a[i] else a[i]:=-a[i];`

   Expressions are non parallelisable if they include function calls.

The dual compilation strategy allows the same linguistic construct to be used in recursive function definitions and parallel data selection.

Use of boolean mask vectors

In array programming many operations can be efficiently be expressed in terms of boolean mask vectors. Given the declarations:

```
const
       s:array[1..4] of string[8]=('dog','fish','bee','beans');
       i:array[1..4] of integer=(1,2,3,4);
       r:array[1..4] of real=(0.5,1.0,2.0,4.0);
       b:array[1..4] of boolean=(false,true,false,true);
var
       c:array[1..4] of complex;
```

and if c is intialised to cmplx(1,0.5), then the statements

```
write (b,i and b, r and b);
write(s:12, (s and b):12 );
write(c and b);
```

will output

```
       false         true         false         true
           0            2             0            4
           0            1             0            4
         dog         fish           bee        beans
                     fish                      beans
         0j0       1j5e-1           0j0       1j5e-1
```

and operations using boolean arrays are particularly usefull in performing parallel selection operations on arrays. For numeric types, they commpile efficiently to SIMD code. Anding a value with boolean true leaves the value unchanged, anding with false returns a null element.

[2]This compilation strategy requires that true is equivalent to -1 and false to 0. This is typically the representation of booleans returned by vector comparison instructions on SIMD instruction sets. In Vector Pascal this representation is used generally and in consequence, `true<false`.

Table 3.2: Null elements for boolean masking

Type	Null Element
Numbers	0
Strings	empty string
Booleans	false

Table 3.3: Multiplicative operators

Operator	Left	Right	Result	Effect of a `op` b
`*`, $\times$	integer	integer	integer	multiply
	string	integer	string	replicate, 'ab'*2 ='abab'
	real	real	real	multiply
	complex	complex	complex	multiply
/	integer	integer	real	division
	real	real	real	division
	complex	complex	complex	division
`div`, $\div$	integer	integer	integer	division
`mod`	integer	integer	integer	remainder
`and`	boolean	boolean	boolean	logical and
`shr`	integer	integer	integer	shift a by b bits right
`shl`	integer	integer	integer	shift a by b bits left
`in`, $\in$	t	`set of` t	boolean	true if a is member of b

3.1.7 Factor

A factor is an expression that optionally performs exponentiation. Vector Pascal supports exponentiation either by integer exponents or by real exponents. A number x can be raised to an integral power y by using the construction x `pow` y. A number can be raised to an arbitrary real power by the `**` operator. The result of `**` is always real valued.

<expop>	'pow' '**'

<factor>	<unary expression> [<expop> <unary expression>]

3.1.8 Multiplicative expressions

Multiplicative expressions consist of factors linked by the multiplicative operators `*`, $\times$, `/`, `div`, $\div$`,`, `mod`, `shr`, `shl` `and`. The use of these operators is summarised in table 3.3.

Table 3.4: Addition operations

	Left	Right	Result	Effect of a op b
+	integer	integer	integer	sum of a and b
	real	real	real	sum of a and b
	complex	complex	complex	sum of a and b
	set	set	set	union of a and b
	string	string	string	concatenate a with b 'ac'+'de'='acde'
-	integer	integer	integer	result of subtracting b from a
	real	real	real	result of subtracting b from a
	complex	complex	complex	result of subtracting b from a
	set	set	set	complement of b relative to a
`+:`	0..255	0..255	0..255	saturated + clipped to 0..255
	-128..127	-128..127	-128..127	saturated + clipped to -128..127
`-:`	0..255	0..255	0..255	saturated - clipped to 0..255
	-128..127	-128..127	-128..127	saturated - clipped to -128..127
`min`	integer	integer	integer	returns the lesser of the numbers
	real	real	real	returns the lesser of the numbers
`max`	integer	integer	integer	returns the greater of the numbers
	real	real	real	returns the greater of the numbers
`or`	boolean	boolean	boolean	logical or
`><`	set	set	set	symetric difference

<multop>	'*'
	'×'
	'/'
	'div'
	'÷'
	'shr'
	'shl'
	'and'
	'mod'

<multiplicative expression>	<factor> [<multop> <factor>]*
	<factor>'in'<multiplicative expression>

3.1.9 Additive expressions

An additive expression allows multiplicative expressions to be combined using the addition operators `+, -, or, +:,max, min, -:, ><`. The additive operations are summarised in table3.4 .

Table 3.5: Relational operators

<	Less than
>	Greater than
<=	Less than or equal to
>=	Greater than or equal to
<>	Not equal to
=	Equal to

<addop>	'+'
	'-'
	'or'
	'max'
	'min'
	'+:'
	'-:'

<additive expression>	<multiplicative expression> [<addop> <multiplicative expression>]*

<expression>	<additive expression> <relational operator> <expression>

3.1.10 Expressions

An expression can optionally involve the use of a relational operator to compare the results of two additive expressions. Relational operators always return boolean results and are listed in table 3.5.

3.1.11 Operator overloading

The dyadic operators can be extended to operate on new types by operator overloading. Figure 3.1 shows how arithmetic on the type `complex` required by Extended Pascal [16] is defined in Vector Pascal. Each operator is associated with a semantic function and if it is a non-relational operator, an identity element. The operator symbols must be drawn from the set of predefined Vector Pascal operators, and when expressions involving them are parsed, priorities are inherited from the predefined operators. The type signature of the operator is deduced from the type of the function[3].

<operator-declaration>	'operator' 'cast' '=' <identifier>
	'operator' <dyadicop> '=' <identifier>','<identifier>
	'operator' <relational operator> '=' <identifier>

When parsing expressions, the compiler first tries to resolve operations in terms of the predefined operators of the language, taking into account the stan-

[3] Vector Pascal allows function results to be of any non-procedural type.

```
interface
  type
    Complex = record data :  array [0..1] of real ;
    end ;

  var
     complexzero, complexone : complex;

  function real2cmplx ( realpart :real ):complex ;
  function cmplx ( realpart ,imag :real ):complex ;
  function complex_add ( A ,B :Complex ):complex ;
  function complex_conjugate ( A :Complex ):complex ;
  function complex_subtract ( A ,B :Complex ):complex ;
  function complex_multiply ( A ,B :Complex ):complex ;
  function complex_divide ( A ,B :Complex ):complex ;
    { Standard operators on complex numbers }
    { symbol function identity element }
    operator + = Complex_add , complexzero ;
    operator / = complex_divide , complexone ;
    operator * = complex_multiply , complexone ;
    operator - = complex_subtract , complexzero ;
    operator cast = real2cmplx ;
```

Note that only the function headers are given here as this code comes from the interface part of the system unit. The function bodies and the initialisation of the variables complexone and complexzero are handled in the implementation part of the unit.

Example 3.1: Defining operations on complex numbers

dard mechanisms allowing operators to work on arrays. Only if these fail does it search for an overloaded operator whose type signature matches the context.

In the example in figure 3.1, complex numbers are defined to be records containing an array of reals, rather than simply as an array of reals. Had they been so defined, the operators `+,*,-,/` on reals would have masked the corresponding operators on complex numbers.

The provision of an identity element for complex addition and subtraction ensures that unary minus, as in $-x$ for x :complex, is well defined, and correspondingly that unary / denotes complex reciprocal. Overloaded operators can be used in array maps and array reductions.

Implicit casts

The Vector Pascal language already contains a number of implicit type conversions that are context determind. An example is the promotion of integers to reals in the context of arithmetic expressions. The set of implicit casts can be added to by declaring an operator to be a cast as is shown in the line:

```
operator cast = real2cmplx ;
```

```
{:tests vector product of  integer vectors                              }
program conf551;
const
      a:array[0..3] of integer=(1,1,2,3);
      b:array[0..3] of integer=(1,2,3,4);
var i:integer;
begin
    i:=a.b;
    if i=21 then
      writeln('PASS   integer vector product allowed')
    else
      writeln('FAIL    integer vector product i=',i)
end.
```

Example 3.2: Example of the inner product operation

Given an implict cast from type $t_0 \rightarrow t_1$, the function associated with the implicit cast is then called on the result of any expression $e : t_0$ whose expression context requires it to be of type t_1.

3.1.12 Vector inner product

The inner product of two vectors is defined as:

$$a.b = \sum_i a_i \times b_i$$

or in Vector Pascal notation: `a.b = \+ a*b` . Vector Pascal supports this inner product operation on any pair of vectors with the following properties:

1. The lengths of the vectors must be the same.

2. The types of the vectors must be such that they support the operators + and *.

Inner product can obviously be used on numeric vectors as shown in Example 3.2 but it can also be used with other types for which + and * are defined, as shown in Example 3.3.

The inner product operation is of higher priority than any other. Its arguments must be arrays.

3.1.13 Matrix to Vector Product

Matrix to vector product can be used to carry out generalised linear geometry transforms. We can do this in Vector Pascal if a two dimensional array is used to multiply a one dimensional array, using the dot product operator. If `M` is a two dimensional array and `v` a vector, `M.v` produces the transformed vector. VECTOR

```
{:tests vector product of string and integer                        }
program conf550;
const roman:array[0..4] of string[3]=('C','L','X','V','I');
        num:   array[0..4] of integer  =(1,1,2,0,3);
var s:string[80];
begin
    s:=num.roman;
    if s='CLXXIII' then
        writeln('PASS string integer vector product allowed')
    else
        writeln('FAIL CONF550 string integer vector product s=',s)
end.
```

Example 3.3: Using vector product to format roman numerals

The program matvmult shown in Example 3.4, shows the repeated application of a rotation and translation matrix to the unit x vector. When the matrix

$$\begin{matrix} \frac{1}{\sqrt{2}} & \frac{-1}{\sqrt{2}} & 0 & 0 \\ \frac{1}{\sqrt{2}} & \frac{1}{\sqrt{2}} & 0 & 0 \\ 0 & 0 & 1 & 0.2 \\ 0 & 0 & 0 & 1 \end{matrix}$$

is applied to a vector of the form $[x, y, z, 1]$, it rotates it by 45° and moves it up by 0.2.

Data-flow Hazards

Note that in Example 3.4, one can not simply write `v1:=M.v1`, instead one has to write:

```
v2:=M.v1;
v1:=v2;
```

since the vector `v1` might be changing whilst it was being read. Had the compiler been encountered this statement it would have generated the error messages:

```
 compilation failed
17 : Error  assignment invalid
17 : Error  in primary expression started by m
17 : Error  attempting to reduce rank of variable
17 : Error  data hazard found. Destination v1 is used with
     an index permutation on right hand side of := which
     can cause it to be corrupted.
     You can get round this by assigning to a temporary
     array instead and then assigning the temporary to
     destination v1
```

```
program matvmult;
type vec=array[0..3] of real;
     mat=array[0..3] of vec;
const
   rr2= 0.7071067 ;              { 1/sqrt(2) }
   M:mat=(( rr2,-rr2,0.0,0.0)  , { 45degree spiral matrix }
          (rr2,rr2,0.0,0.0),
          (0.0,0.0,1.0,0.2),
          (0.0,0.0,0.0,1.0));
  v:vec=(1.0,0.0,0.0,1.0);
var v1,v2:vec; i:integer;
begin
  write (M,v);
  v1:=v;
  (* perform 8 45degree rotations *)
  for i:=1 to 8 do begin
     v2:=M.v1;
     v1:=v2;
     write(v1);
  end;
end.
```

produces as output

```
   0.70711    -0.70711     0.00000     0.00000
   0.70711     0.70711     0.00000     0.00000
   0.00000     0.00000     1.00000     0.20000
   0.00000     0.00000     0.00000     1.00000
   1.00000     0.00000     0.00000     1.00000
   0.70711     0.70711     0.20000     1.00000
   0.00000     1.00000     0.40000     1.00000
  -0.70711     0.70711     0.60000     1.00000
  -1.00000    -0.00000     0.80000     1.00000
  -0.70711    -0.70711     1.00000     1.00000
  -0.00000    -1.00000     1.20000     1.00000
   0.70711    -0.70711     1.40000     1.00000
   1.00000    -0.00000     1.60000     1.00000
```

Example 3.4: Using a spiral rotation matrix to operate on the unit x vector.

A check for data-flow hazards is applied to all array assignment statements. If array expressions could all be evaluated in parallel, then there would be no hazards. The problem arises because only simple array expressions can be evaluated entirely in parallel. In other cases the array assignment has to be broken down by the compiler into a sequence of steps. This gives rise to the danger that an array location may be altered by an early step prior to it being used a source of data by a subsequent step.

In most cases there will be no problem even where the destination vector appears on the right hand side of an assignment. Thus:

```
M:=M+v;
```

for some matrix `M` and vector `v`, is ok, since here each element of `M` depends only on its own prior value. However for `v1:=M.v1`, we have the equations

$$v1_0 = \sum_{j=0}^{3} M_{0j} v1_j \tag{3.1}$$

$$v1_1 = \sum_{j=0}^{3} M_{1j} v1_j \tag{3.2}$$

In which ever order the code for these equations is evaluated, either $v1_0$ or $v1_1$will be altered before it is used in the other equation.

3.1.14 Matrix to Matrix multiplication

VECTOR

The dot operator can be used between matrices to perform matrix multiplication as illustrated in Example 3.5. This applies the standard equation for matrix multiplication:

$$c_{ik} = \sum_{s=1}^{p} a_{is} b_{sk} \tag{3.3}$$

where A is of order $(m \times p)$and B is of order $(p \times n)$ to give a resulting matrix C of order $(m \times n)$.

```
program matmmult;
const
   A:array[1..2,1..3] of integer=((3,1,2),
                                  (2,1,3));
   B:array[1..3,1..2] of integer=((1,2),
                                  (3,1),
                                  (2,3));
var C:array[1..2,1..2] of integer;
begin
  C:=A.B;
  writeln(C);
end.
```

Produces output

```
         10          13
         11          14
```

Example 3.5: Matrix by matrix multiplication.

3.2 Statements

<statement>	<variable>':='<expression>
	<procedure statement>
	<empty statement>
	'goto' <label>;
	'exit'['('<expression>')']
	'begin' <statement>[;<statement>]*'end'
	'if'<expression>'then'<statement>['else'<statement>]
	<case statement>
	'for' <variable>:= <expression> 'to' <expression> 'do' <statement>
	'for' <variable>:= <expression> 'downto' <expression> 'do' <statement>
	'repeat' <statement> 'until' <expression>
	'with' <record variable> 'do' < statement>
	<io statement>
	'while' <expression> 'do' <statement>

3.2.1 Assignment

An assignment replaces the current value of a variable by a new value specified by an expression. The assignment operator is :=. Standard Pascal allows assignment of whole arrays. Vector Pascal extends this to allow consistent use of mixed rank expressions on the right hand side of an assignment. Given

```
r0:real; r1:array[0..7] of real;
r2:array[0..7,0..7] of real
```

then we can write

1. `r1:= r2[3]; { supported in standard Pascal }`
2. `r1:= /2; { assign 0.5 to each element of r1 }`
3. `r2:= r1*3; { assign 1.5 to every element of r2}`
4. `r1:= \+ r2; { r1 gets the totals along the rows of r2}`
5. `r1:= r1+r2[1];{ r1 gets the corresponding elements of row 1 of r2 added to it}`

The assignment of arrays is a generalisation of what standard Pascal allows. Consider the first examples above, they are equivalent to:

1. `for i:=0 to 7 do r1[i]:=r2[3,i];`
2. `for i:=0 to 7 do r1[i]:=/2;`
3. ```
   for i:=0 to 7 do
   for j:=0 to 7 do r2[i,j]:=r1[j]*3;
   ```
4. ```
   for i:=0 to 7 do
   begin
    t:=0;
    for j:=7 downto 0 do t:=r2[i,j]+t;
    r1[i]:=t;
   end;
   ```
5. `for i:=0 to 7 do r1[i]:=r1[i]+r2[1,i];`

In other words the compiler has to generate an implicit loop over the elements of the array being assigned to and over the elements of the array acting as the data-source. In the above `i,j,t` are assumed to be temporary variables not referred to anywhere else in the program. The loop variables are called implicit indices and may be accessed using `iota`.

The variable on the left hand side of an assignment defines an array context within which expressions on the right hand side are evaluated. Each array context has a rank given by the number of dimensions of the array on the left hand side. A scalar variable has rank 0. Variables occurring in expressions with an array context of rank r must have r or fewer dimensions. The n bounds of any n dimensional array variable, with $n \leq r$ occurring within an expression evaluated in an array context of rank r must match with the rightmost n bounds of the array on the left hand side of the assignment statement.

Where a variable is of lower rank than its array context, the variable is replicated to fill the array context. This is shown in examples 2 and 3 above. Because the rank of any assignment is constrained by the variable on the left hand side, no temporary arrays, other than machine registers, need be allocated to store the intermediate array results of expressions.

3.2.2 Procedure statement

A procedure statement executes a named procedure. A procedure statement may, in the case where the named procedure has formal parameters, contain a list of actual parameters. These are substituted in place of the formal parameters contained in the declaration. Parameters may be value parameters or variable parameters.

Semantically the effect of a value parameter is that a copy is taken of the actual parameter and this copy substituted into the body of the procedure. Value parameters may be structured values such as records and arrays. For scalar values, expressions may be passed as actual parameters. Array expressions are not currently allowed as actual parameters.

A variable parameter is passed by reference, and any alteration of the formal parameter induces a corresponding change in the actual parameter. Actual variable parameters must be variables.

<parameter>	<variable>	for formal parameters declared as var
	<expression>	for other formal parameters

<procedure statement>	<identifier>
	<identifier> '(' <parameter> [','<parameter>]* ')'

Examples

1. `printlist;`

2. `compare(avec,bvec,result);`

3.2.3 Goto statement

A goto statement transfers control to a labelled statement. The destination label must be declared in a label declaration. It is illegal to jump into or out of a procedure.

Example `goto 99;`

3.2.4 Exit Statement

An exit statement transfers control to the calling point of the current procedure or function. If the exit statement is within a function then the exit statement can have a parameter: an expression whose value is returned from the function.

Examples

1. `exit;`

2. `exit(5);`

3.2.5 Compound statement

A list of statements separated by semicolons may be grouped into a compound statement by bracketing them with `begin` and `end` .

Example `begin a:=x*3; b:=sqrt a end;`

3.2.6 If statement

The basic control flow construct is the if statement. If the boolean expression between `if` and `then` is true then the statement following `then` is followed. If it is false and an else part is present, the statement following `else` is executed.

3.2.7 Case statement

The case statement specifies an expression which is evaluated and which must be of integral or ordinal type. Dependent upon the value of the expression control transfers to the statement labelled by the matching constant.

<case statement>	'case'<expression>'of'<case actions>'end'

<case actions>	<case list> <case list> 'else' <statement> <case list> 'otherwise' <statement>

<case list>	<case list element>[';'<case list element.]*

<case list element>	<case label>[',' <case label>]':'<statement>

<case label>	<constant> <constant> '..' <constant>

Examples

```
case i of
1:s:=abs s;
2:s:= sqrt s;
3:  s:=0
end
```

```
case c of
'a':write('A');
'b','B':write('B');
'A','C'..'Z','c'..'z':write(' ');
end
```

3.2.8 With statement

Within the component statement of the with statement the fields of the record variable can be referred to without prefixing them by the name of the record variable. The effect is to import the component statement into the scope defined by the record variable declaration so that the field-names appear as simple variable names.

Example
```
var s:record x,y:real end;
begin
with s do begin x:=0;y:=1 end ;
end
```

3.2.9 For statement

A for statement executes its component statement repeatedly under the control of an iteration variable. The iteration variable must be of an integral or ordinal type. The variable is either set to count up through a range or down through a range.

```
for i:= e1 to e2 do s
```
is equivalent to
```
i:=e1; temp:=e2;while i<=temp do s;
```
whilst
```
for i:= e1 downto e2 do s
```
is equivalent to
```
i:=e1; temp:=e2;while i>= temp do s;
```

3.2.10 While statement

A while statement executes its component statement whilst its boolean expression is true. The statement
```
while e do s
```
is equivalent to
```
10:  if not e then goto 99; s; goto 10; 99:
```

3.2.11 Repeat statement

A repeat statement executes its component statement at least once, and then continues to execute the component statement until its component expression becomes true.
```
repeat s until e
```
is equivalent to
```
10:  s;if e then goto 99; goto 10;99:
```

3.3 Input Output

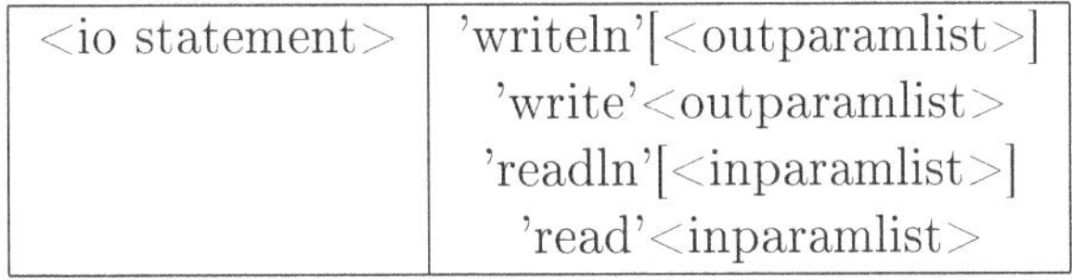

<io statement>	'writeln'[<outparamlist>] 'write'<outparamlist> 'readln'[<inparamlist>] 'read'<inparamlist>

<outparamlist>	'('<outparam>[','<outparam>]*')'

<outparam>	<expression>[':' <expression>] [':'<expression>]

<inparamlist>	'('<variable>[','<variable>]*')'

Input and output are supported from and to the console and also from and to files.

3.3.1 Input

The basic form of input is the **read** statement. This takes a list of parameters the first of which may optionally be a file variable. If this file variable is present it is the input file. In the absence of a leading file variable the input file is the standard input stream. The parameters take the form of variables into which appropriate translations of textual representations of values in the file are read. The statement

`read(a,b,c)`

where *a,b,c* are non file parameters is exactly equivalent to the sequence of statements

`read(a);read(b);read(c)`

The **readln** statement has the same effect as the read statement but finishes by reading a new line from the input file. The representation of the new line is operating system dependent. The statement

`readln(a,b,c)`

where *a,b,c* are non file parameters is thus exactly equivalent to the sequence of statements

`read(a);read(b);read(c);readln;`

Allowed typed for read statements are: integers, reals, strings and enumerated types.

3.3.2 Output

The basic form of output is the **write** statement. This takes a list of parameters the first of which may optionally be a file variable. If this file variable is present it is the output file. In the absence of a leading file variable the output file is the console. The parameters take the form of expressions whose values whose textual representations are written to the output file. The statement

`write(a,b,c)`

where *a,b,c* are non file parameters is exactly equivalent to the sequence of statements

`write(a);write(b);write(c)`

The **writeln** statement has the same effect as the write statement but finishes by writing a new line to the output file. The representation of the new line is operating system dependent. The statement

`writeln(a,b,c)`

where *a,b,c* are non file parameters is thus exactly equivalent to the sequence of statements

`write(a);write(b);write(c);writeln;`

Allowed types for write statements are integers, reals, strings and enumerated types.

Parameter formating

A non file parameter can be followed by up to two integer expressions prefixed by colons which specify the field widths to be used in the output. The write parameters can thus have the following forms:
e e:*m e*:*m*:*n*

1. If *e* is an integral type its decimal expansion will be written preceeded by sufficient blanks to ensure that the total textual field width produced is not less than *m*.

2. If *e* is a real its decimal expansion will be written preceeded by sufficient blanks to ensure that the total textual field width produced is not less than *m*. If *n* is present the total number of digits after the decimal point will be *n*. If *n* is omitted then the number will be written out in exponent and mantissa form with 6 digits after the decimal point

3. If *e* is boolean the strings 'true' or 'false' will be written into a field of width not less than m.

4. If *e* If the value of e is a string-type value with a length of *n*, the default value of *m* shall be n. The representation shall consist of

```
if m > n,
  (m - n) spaces,
if n > 0,
  the first through n-th characters of the value of e in that order.
if 1 <= m <= n,
  the first through m-th characters in that order.
if m = 0,
  no characters.
```

4 Programs, Units and Libraries

Vector Pascal supports the popular system of separate compilation units found in Turbo Pascal. A compilation unit can be either a program, a unit or a library.

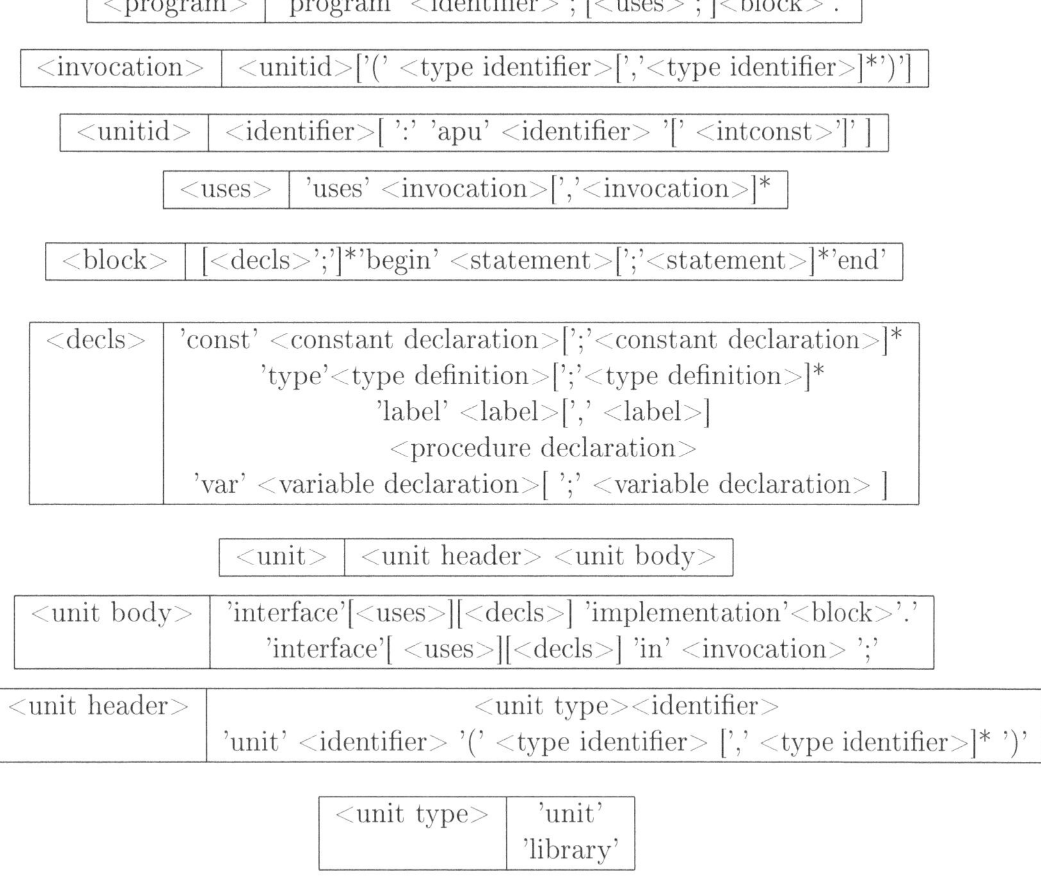

<program>	'program' <identifier>';'[<uses>';']<block>'.'

<invocation>	<unitid>['(' <type identifier>[','<type identifier>]*')']

<unitid>	<identifier>[':' 'apu' <identifier> '[' <intconst>']']

<uses>	'uses' <invocation>[','<invocation>]*

<block>	[<decls>';']*'begin' <statement>[';'<statement>]*'end'

<decls>	'const' <constant declaration>[';'<constant declaration>]*
	'type'<type definition>[';'<type definition>]*
	'label' <label>[',' <label>]
	<procedure declaration>
	'var' <variable declaration>[';' <variable declaration>]

<unit>	<unit header> <unit body>

<unit body>	'interface'[<uses>][<decls>] 'implementation'<block>'.'
	'interface'[<uses>][<decls>] 'in' <invocation> ';'

<unit header>	<unit type><identifier>
	'unit' <identifier> '(' <type identifier> [',' <type identifier>]* ')'

<unit type>	'unit'
	'library'

An executable compilation unit must be declared as a program. The program can use several other compilation units all of which must be either units or libraries. The units or libraries that it directly uses are specified by a list of identifiers in an optional use list at the start of the program. A unit or library has two declaration portions and an executable block.

4.1 The export of identifiers from units

The first declaration portion is the interface part and is preceded by the reserved word `interface`.

The definitions in the interface section of unit files constitute a sequence of enclosing scopes, such that successive units in the with list ever more closely contain the program itself. Thus when resolving an identifier, if the identifier can not be resolved within the program scope, the declaration of the identifier within the interface section of the rightmost unit in the uses list is taken as the defining occurrence. It follows that rightmost occurrence of an identifier definition within the interface parts of units on the uses list overrides all occurrences in interface parts of units to its left in the uses list.

The implementation part of a unit consists of declarations, preceded by the reserved word `implementation` that are private to the unit with the exception that a function or procedure declared in an interface context can omit the procedure body, provided that the function or procedure is redeclared in the implementation part of the unit. In that case the function or procedure heading given in the interface part is taken to refer to the function or procedure of the same name whose body is declared in the implementation part. The function or procedure headings sharing the same name in the interface and implementation parts must correspond with respect to parameter types, parameter order and, in the case of functions, with respect to return types.

A unit may itself contain a use list, which is treated in the same way as the use lists of a program. That is to say, the use list of a unit makes accessible identifiers declared within the interface parts of the units named within the use list to the unit itself.

4.1.1 The export of Operators from units

A unit can declare a type and export operators for that type.

4.2 Unit parameterisation and generic functions

Standard Pascal provides es some limited support for polymorphism in its `read` and `write` functions. Vector Pascal allows the writing of polymorphic functions and procedures through the use of parameteric units.

A unit header can include an optional parameter list. The parameters identifiers which are interepreted as type names. These can be used to declare polymorphic procedures and functions, parameterised by these type names. This is shown in figure 4.1.

4.3 The invocation of programs and units

Programs and units contain an executable block. The rules for the execution of these are as follows:

1. When a program is invoked by the operating system, the units or libraries in its use list are invoked first followed by the executable block of the program itself.
2. When a unit or library is invoked, the units or libraries in its use list are invoked first followed by the executable block of the unit or library itself.

```
unit genericsort(t) ;
interface
type
    dataarray ( n ,m :integer )=array [n ..m ] of t ;
procedure sort ( var a :dataarray ); (see Figure 4.2 )

implementation

procedure sort ( var a :dataarray ); (see Figure 4.2 )
begin
end .
```

Example 4.1: A polymorphic sorting unit.

```
procedure  sort (  var  a :dataarray );
var
    Let i, j ∈ integer;
    Let temp ∈ t;
begin
    for i← a.n to a.m - 1 do
        for j← a.n to a.m - 1 do
        if a[j] > a[j+1] then begin begin
                temp← a[j];
                a[j] ← a[j+1];
                a[j+1] ← temp;
            end ;
end ;
```

Example 4.2: procedure sort

3. The order of invocation of the units or libraries in a use list is left to right with the exception provided by rule 4.

4. No unit or library may be invoked more than once.

Note that rule 4 implies that a unit x to the right of a unit y within a use list, may be invoked before the unit y, if the unit y or some other unit to y's left names x in its use list.

Note that the executable part of a library will only be invoked if the library in the context of a Vector Pascal program. If the library is linked to a main program in some other language, then the library and any units that it uses will not be invoked. Care should thus be taken to ensure that Vector Pascal libraries to be called from main programs written in other languages do not depend upon initialisation code contained within the executable blocks of units.

4.4 The compilation of programs and units.

When the compiler processes the use list of a unit or a program then, from left to right, for each identifier in the use list it attempts to find an already compiled unit whose filename prefix is equal to the identifier. If such a file exists, it then looks for a source file whose filename prefix is equal to the identifier, and whose suffix is `.pas`. If such a file exists and is older than the already compiled file, the already compiled unit, the compiler loads the definitions contained in the pre-compiled unit. If such a file exists and is newer than the pre-compiled unit, then the compiler attempts to re-compile the unit source file. If this recompilation proceeds without the detection of any errors the compiler loads the definitions of the newly compiled unit. The definitions in a unit are saved to a file with the suffix `.mpu`, and prefix given by the unit name. The compiler also generates an assembler file for each unit compiled.

4.5 Instantiation of parametric units

Instantiation of a parametric unit refers to the process by which the unbound type variables introduced in the parameter list of the unit are bound to actual types. In Vector Pascal all instantiation of parametric units and all type polymorphism are resolved at compile time. Two mechanisms are provided by which a parametric unit may be instantiated.

4.5.1 Direct instantiation

If a generic unit is invoked in the use list of a program or unit, then the unit name must be followed by a list of type identifiers. Thus given the generic sort unit in figure 4.1, one could instantiate it to sort arrays of reals by writing

uses *genericsort*(*real*);

at the head of a program. Following this header, the procedure ***sort*** would be declared as operating on arrays of reals.

4.5.2 Indirect instantiation

A named unit file can indirectly instantiate a generic unit where its unit body uses the syntax

'interface' <uses><decls> 'in' <invocation> ';'

For example

unit *intsort* ;
interface
  in *genericsort* (*integer*);

would create a named unit to sort integers. The naming of the parametric units allows more than one instance of a given parametric unit to be used in a program. The generic sort unit could be used to provide both integer and real sorting procedures. The different variants of the procedures would be distinquished by using fully qualified names - e.g., *intsort.sort*.

4.6 The System Unit

All programs and units include by default the unit system.pas as an implicit member of their with list. This contains declarations of private run time routines needed by Vector Pascal and also the following user accessible routines.

`function abs` Return absolute value of a real or integer.

`procedure append(var f:file);` This opens a file in append mode.

`function arctan(x:Real):Real;`

`procedure assign(var f:file;var fname:string);` Associates a file name with a file. It does not open the file.

`procedure blockread(var f:file;var buf;count:integer; var resultcount:integer);` Trys to read count bytes from the file into the buffer. Resultcount contains the number actually read.

`LatexCommand \index{blockwrite}procedure blockwrite(var f:file;var buf;count:integer; var resultcount:integer);` Write count bytes from the buffer. Resultcount gives the number actually read.

`procedure close`(var f:file); Closes a file.

`function eof`(var f:file):boolean; True if we are at the end of file f.

`procedure erase`(var f:file); Delete file f.

`function eoln`(var f:file):boolean; True if at the end of a line.

`function exp`(d:real):real; Return e^x

`function filesize`(var f: fileptr):integer; Return number of bytes in a file.

`function filepos`(var f:fileptr):integer; Return current position in a file.

`procedure freemem(var p:pointer; num:integer);` Free num bytes of heap store. Called by dispose.

bold procedure getmem(var p:pointer; num:integer); Allocate num bytes of heap. Called by new.

`procedure gettime(var hour,min,sec,hundredth:integer);` Return time of day.

Return the integer part of r as a real.

`function ioresult:integer;` Returns a code indicating if the previous file operation completed ok. Zero if no error occurred.

`function length(var s:string):integer;` Returns the length of s.

`procedure pascalexit(code:integer);` Terminate the program with code.

Time in 1/100 seconds since program started.

`function random:integer;` Returns a random integer.

`procedure randomize;` Assign a new time dependent seed to the random number generator.

`procedure reset(var f:file);` Open a file for reading.

`procedure rewrite(var f :file);` Open a file for writing.

`function trunc(r:real):integer;` Truncates a real to an integer.

4.6.1 System unit constants

```
BLANK          =' ';
maxint  = 2147483647;
pi  = 3.14159265358979323855;
MAXSTRING { longest allowed string}
MAXREAL =3.4E38;
MINREAL =1.18E-38;

EPSREAL { smallest increment of reals around 0 }
MAXDOUBLE =1.79E308;
MINDOUBLE =2.23E-308;
MAXCHAR =chr(65535);
MINCHAR =chr(0);
NILSTR ='';

minint64 =-9223372036854775807;
maxint64 =9223372036854775807;
```

4.7 Libraries, static and dynamic

4.7.1 Linking to external libraries

It is possible to specify to which external libraries - that is to say libraries written in another languge, a program should be linked by placing in the main program linkage directives. For example

```
{$linklib ncurses}
```

would cause the program to be linked to the ncurses library.

4.7.2 The export of procedures from libraries.

If a compilation unit is prefixed by the reserved word `library` rather than the words `program` or `unit`, then the procedure and function declarations in its interface part are made accessible to routines written in other languages.

4.7.3 Creating libraries

Depending on the linking that you do these Vector Pascal libraries can either be staticly linked into a C program, or can form a Dynamic Link Library (DLL) which can be linked at runtime to the C code. What follows are two examples of how to do this.

Static Libraries

Static libraries can be used in either Linux or Windows systems. Building and using a library involves several stages and should be controlled by the use of make files.

Here is an example library:

```
library examplelib;
interface

 procedure exampleproc;

implementation

 procedure exampleproc;
 begin
  writeln(' procedure in library called');
 end;
end.
```

and here is an example C program that calls the library:

```
#include<stdio.h>
main(argc, argv)
{
  extern void examplelib_exampleproc();
  printf("start of C program \n");
  dllinit();                       /* initialise the pascal runtime library */
  examplelib_exampleproc();        /* call the library procedure */
  printf("end of C program\n");
}
```

In order to use the library from C we must do the following:

1. Compile the library to assembler language.
2. Use the gnu tools to assemble this to an object file.

3. Create an object file version of the pascal runtime library.
4. Link both of these with the C program that is going to use the library.

The steps could be performed by the following makefile:

```
CFLAGS=-g

all: uselib
     uselib

examplelib.s: examplelib.pas
     vpc examplelib -S -Aexamplelib.s -cpugnuPentium
#    complile the library to assembly language

examplelib.o: examplelib.s
     gcc $(CFLAGS)    -c examplelib.s

rtl.o: rtl.c
     gcc $(CFLAGS) -DBUILD_DLL   -c rtl.c
# compile it in a form suitable for use in a library

rtl.c: ../../mmpc/rtl.c
     cp ../../mmpc/rtl.c rtl.c
# get a copy of the pascal run time library
# from wherever we have installed the vector pascal system

uselib: uselib.c examplelib.o rtl.o
     gcc $(CFLAGS) uselib.c rtl.o examplelib.o -o uselib
# link the C program with the examplelib
```

DLLs

DLLs or Dynamic Link Libraries are a type of Windows file that can be linked to at runtime. Building them is more complex than a static library as one needs to write a .def file which defines which functions are to be exported from the DLL, and one must also build a stub library to which the main program can be linked. One can use the gnu `dlltool` to build the stub library.

We illustrate the process with a similar example. First the C program:

```
#include<stdio.h>
main(argc, argv)
{
printf("start\n");
dllinit();
exampledll_exampleproc();
}
```

Next the example DLL in Pascal:

```
library exampledll;
interface
 procedure exampleproc;
implementation
 procedure exampleproc;
 begin
  writeln(' procedure in dll called');
 end;
end.
```

We now provide a file exampledll.def file which tells the gnu `dlltool` which functions we want to export:

```
EXPORTS
exampledll_exampleproc
dllinit
```

Finally the make file:

```
CFLAGS=-mno-cygwin
# specify that cygwin gcc is to rely on the windows built in C libraries

all: usedll.exe exampledll.dll
     usedll

exampledll.s: exampledll.pas
     vpc exampledll -S -Aexampledll.s -U -cpugnuPentium

exampledll.o: exampledll.s
    gcc $(CFLAGS) -DBUILD_DLL   -c exampledll.s

rtl.o: rtl.c
    gcc $(CFLAGS) -DBUILD_DLL   -c rtl.c
# compile it in a form suitable for use in a dll

rtl.c: ../../mmpc/rtl.c
    cp ../../mmpc/rtl.c rtl.c
# get a copy of the pascal run time library

exports.o: exampledll.a

exampledll.a: exampledll.def makefile
     dlltool -v -e exports.o -l exampledll.a -d exampledll.def -D exampledll.dll exampledll.o rtl.o
# Note that you must use the -D option to tell dlltool the name of the dll you will build
#     this also reads in the .def file it produces exampledll.a with which
#     you statically link your c program ( it contains stubs to the real dynamic fns )

exampledll.dll: exports.o rtl.o exampledll.o
     gcc $(CFLAGS) -shared exports.o rtl.o exampledll.o   -o exampledll.dll
# build the dll using the export spec produced by dlltool
```

```
usedll.o: usedll.c
    gcc $(CFLAGS) -c usedll.c
# compile the c program to an object file

usedll.exe: usedll.o exampledll.a
    gcc $(CFLAGS) usedll.c exampledll.a -o usedll
# link the c program with the exampledll stub library
```

4.7.4 Cross Language Parameter Passing

When calling Pascal from C observe the following rules:

- Atomic values of type integer and real can be passed as value parameters. Pascal type `real` corresponds to C type `float`.
- Composite values such as records arrays or strings should be passed as pascal var parameters, and in C call the address of the composite item must be passed.
- Strings in Vector Pascal are stored in 16 bit unicode preceded by a 16 bit length word. C strings are stored as arrays ASCII of bytes. If a Pascal procedure requires a string parameter, then the C code calling it must pack the string into an array of `short`.

Thus a Pascal procedure exported from library mylib and declared as follows

```
type intarray=array[0..99] of integer;
procedure foo(var s:string; r:real; var f:intarray);
```

would have the C prototype

```
extern void mylib_foo(short *, float, int *);
```

5 Implementation issues

The compiler is implemented in java to ease portability between operating systems.

5.1 Using Unicode with Vector Pascal

ISO Pascal is defined using an alphabet of symbols all of which can be represented with ASCII. Vector Pascal uses Unicode to permit a wider range of symbols to be used in programs.

Programs should be submitted to the compiler in UTF-8 encoded Unicode. Since the 7 bit ASCII is a subset of UTF-8, all valid ASCII encoded Vector Pascal programs are also valid UTF-8 programs.

5.1.1 Letter based Identifiers

ISO Pascal allows the Latin letters A-Z to be used in identifiers. Vector Pascal extends this by allowing letters from the Greek, Cyrillic, Katakana and Hiragana character sets.

Alphabet	Position	glyph	code
Greek	low	Α	0391
	high	Ω	03a9
Cyrillic	low	А	0410
	high	Я	042f
Katakana	low	ア	30a0
	high	ヺ	30fa
Hiragana	low	ぁ	3041
	high	ゔ	0394

Treatment of identifiers is case indifferent, in that upper case and lower case versions of a given letter are treated as equivalent. Thus the identifier "d" may al so be written "?". Identifiers drawn from these alphabets can be strings of letters or digits starting with a letter.

5.1.2 Ideographic identifiers

Vector Pascal allows the use of Ideographs drawn from the unified Chinese, Japanese and Korean sets (Unicode range 4e00-9fff) to act as identifiers.

5.1.3 Special Symbols

When using Unicode certain mathematical operations that are encoded as a sequence of ASCII characters can be represented as a single Unicode character.

Operation	ASCII form	Extended form	Unicode
Set membership	in	$\in$	2208
Assignment	:=	$\leftarrow$	2190
Integer division	div	$\div$	00f7
Nary summation	\+	$\sum$	2211
Nary product	*	$\prod$	220f
Square root	sqrt	$\surd$	221a
Less than or equal	<=	$\leq$	2264
Greater than or equal	>=	$\geq$	2265
Not equal	< >	$\neq$	2260
Negation	not	$\neg$	00ac
Logical and	and	$\wedge$	2227
Logical or	or	$\vee$	2228
Multiplication	*	$\times$	2715
Index generation	iota	$\imath$	2373

Example The following shows the use of Unicode operators in place of the Ascii ones used on early releases of Vector Pascal.

```
Program proddemo;
{ prints the product and square root of the integers 1..5 }
Var a:array[1..5] of Integer; Y:integer;
Begin
  { unicode version}
  a ← ⍳ 0; { form integers from 1 to 5 }
  Writeln(a);
  Y ← ∏ a; { get their product }
  Writeln( y, √y);
  { now using ascii }
  a:= iota 0;
  writeln(a);
  y:= \* a;
  writeln (y, sqrt(y));
End.
```

Characters The built in char type in Pascal is represented with 16 bits in Vector Pascal. This allows any Unicode character to be handled.

Strings Strings are held as arrays of char with a length word held in the first character. This is a simple extension of the mechanism used in Turbo Pascal. It potentially allows strings to be up to 65535 characters long. The type STRING written without a length specification stands for a string of length MAXSTRING.

Read When reading strings or characters from a text file, conversion is automatically performed from utf-8 to Unicode format.

Write When characters or strings are output to a text file, they are converted from the internal Unicode format to the utf-8 format.

5.2 Invoking the compiler

The compiler is invoked with the command

```
vpc filename
```

where filename is the name of a Pascal program or unit. For example

```
vpc test
```

will compile the program test.pas and generate an executable file `test`, (`test.exe` under windows).

The command `vpc` is a shell script which invokes the java runtime system to execute a `.jar` file containing the compiler classes. Instead of running vpc the java interpreter can be directly invoked as follows

```
java -jar mmpc.jar filename
```

The `vpc` script sets various compiler options appropriate to the operating system being used.

5.2.1 Environment variable

The environment variable `mmpcdir` must be set to the directory which contains the `mmpc.jar` file, the runtime library `rtl.o` and the `system.pas` file.

5.2.2 Compiler options

The following flags can be supplied to the compiler :

`-Afilename` Defines the assembler file to be created. In the absence of this option the assembler file is `p.asm`.

`-BOEHM` Causes the program to be linked with the Boehm conservative garbage collector.

`-cores`n generate code for n cores executing in parallel.

`-cpuCGFLAG` Specifies the code generator to be used. Currently the code generators shown in table 5.1 are supported. Note that late model Intel processors operating in 64 bit mode can also accept code compiled with the Opteron instructionset.

`-d`*dirname* Defines the directory in which to find `rtl.o` and `system.pas`.

-D<symbol> Define compiler pre-processor flag for conditional compilation

`-fFORMAT` Specifies the object format to be generated by the assembler. The object formats currently used are elf when compiling under Unix or when compiling under windows using the cygwin version of the gcc linker, or coff when using the djgpp version of the gcc linker. for other formats consult the NASM documentation.

`-help` print out details of command usage.

`-inter` generate an intermediate ilc file for the syntax tree.

`-L` Causes a latex listing to be produced of all files compiled. The level of detail can be controled using the codes -L1 to -L3, otherwise the maximum detail level is used.

`-nobalance` switches off cannonical re-ordering of expression trees.

`-nolink` switches off linking so that a .o file is generated .

`-NOVPWORDS` Allows Vector Pascal reserved words that do not occur in Turbo or in Extended Pascal to be used as identifiers. This may be useful for backward compatibility.

`-OPT`*n* Sets the optimisation level attempted. -OPT0 is no optimisation, -OPT3 is the maximum level attempted. The default is -OPT1.

`-oexefile` Causes the linker to output to `exefile` instead of the default output of `p.exe`.

`-S` Suppresses assembly and linking of the program. An assembler file is still generated.

`-T` Run in training mode, do not load any of the pre-learned code generation tactics stored in the .vwu file

`-U` Defines whether references to external procedures in the assembler file should be preceded by an under-bar '_'. This is required for the coff object format but not for elf.

`-V` Causes the code generator to produce a verbose diagnostic listing to `foo.lst` when compiling `foo.pas`.

`-switchon`*n..m* switch on verbose mode between lines *n* and *m* in source when generating code.

Table 5.1: Code generators supported

CGFLAG	description
IA32	generates code for the Intel 486 instruction-set uses the NASM assembler
Pentium	generates code for the Intel P6 with MMX instruction-set uses the NASM assembler
gnuPentium	generates code for the Intel P6 with MMX instruction-set using the `as` assembler in the gcc package
K6	generates code for the AMD K6 instruction-set, use for Athlon uses the NASM assembler
P3	generates code for the Intel PIII processor family uses the NASM assembler
P4	generates code for the Intel PIV family and Athlon XP uses the NASM assembler
gnuP4	generates code for the Intel PIV family and Athlon XP uses the gas assembler
AVX32	generates 32 bit code for the AVX instructionset uses the NASM assembler
Opteron	generates code for the AMD64 family uses the gas assembler

5.2.3 Dependencies

The Vector Pascal compiler depends upon a number of other utilities which are usually pre-installed on Linux systems, and are freely available for Windows systems.

NASM The net-wide assembler. This is used to convert the output of the code generator to linkable modules. It is freely available on the web for Windows. For the Pentium processor it is possible to use the `as` assembler instead.

gcc The GNU C Compiler, used to compile the run time library and to link modules produced by the assembler to the run time library.

java The java virtual machine must be available to interpret the compiler. There are number of java interpreters and just in time compilers are freely available for Windows.

5.3 Procedure and function mechanism

5.3.1 Requirements

1. Must be able to call C routines as well as Pascal ones.

2. Must establish a name correspondence with C routines that we call externally.

3. Must pass parameters appropriately

4. Must get results back from C routines

Name correspondance

name correspondence with the C routine

Issues here

1. Case of the names

2. allowed characters

3. how are these passed in assembler

Characters and significance

Case is significant both in C, but this is not the case of all languages.

Pascal for instance makes case insignificant, and requires that externals where the case is significant be given a name in quotes for example:

```
procedure close (var f:fileptr);
external name 'pasclose';
```

This allows the external routine to have a different name to the internal representation of it. The allowed characters in a name in Hi are limited to the letters, that means we can not call and C routine with an _ or a digit in its name unless we were to extend the syntax for externals along the above lines.

Assembler representation

In the assembler file, the compiler must list all the externals as follows (note this is the Nasm syntax, it will be different for other assemblers):

```
extern  vconcat
extern  iota
extern  putChar
extern  getNum
extern  getChar
extern  putNum
```

Then we can call them just as if they were declared within this file.

```
call vconcat
```

Underscores

Most 32-bit C compilers share the convention used by 16-bit compilers, that the names of all global symbols (functions or data) they define are formed by prefixing an underscore to the name as it appears in the C program.

However, not all of them do: the 'ELF' specification states that C symbols do **not** have a leading underscore on their assembly-language names.

Thus if you are producing code for Linux, which uses ELF, do not use underscores.

In Vector Pascal the -U flag on the command line selects whether leading underscores are to be generated.

5.3.2 The C calling convention

Before explaining the Vector Pascal function calling technique we present, the simpler technique used in C and that could be used in Pascal if there were no nesting of procedures. The convention used in diagrams in this section is that low addresses are show at the top of the page and high addresses at the bottom.

To call a C function, whether from C or from Pascal the following must be done.

1. The caller pushes the function's parameters on the stack, one after another, in reverse order (right to left, so that the first argument specified to the function is pushed last).
2. The caller then executes a near 'CALL' instruction to pass control to the callee.
3. The callee receives control, and typically (although this is not actually necessary, in functions which do not need to access their parameters) starts by saving the value of 'ESP' in 'EBP' so as to be able to use 'EBP' as a base pointer to find its parameters on the stack. However, the caller was probably doing this too, so part of the calling convention states that 'EBP' must be preserved by any C function. Hence the callee, if it is going to set up 'EBP' as a frame pointer, must push the previous value first.
4. The callee may then access its parameters relative to 'EBP'. The doubleword at '[EBP]' holds the previous value of 'EBP' as it was pushed; the next doubleword, at '[EBP+4]', holds the return address, pushed implicitly by 'CALL'. The parameters start after that, at '[EBP+8]'. The leftmost parameter of the function, since it was pushed last, is accessible at this offset from 'EBP'; the others follow, at successively greater offsets. Thus, in a function such as 'printf' which takes a variable number of parameters, the pushing of the parameters in reverse order means that the function knows where to find its first parameter, which tells it the number and type of the remaining ones.
5. The callee may also wish to decrease 'ESP' further, so as to allocate space on the stack for local variables, which will then be accessible at negative offsets from 'EBP'.

6. The callee, if it wishes to return a value to the caller, should leave the value in 'AL', 'AX' or 'EAX' depending on the size of the value. Floating-point results are typically returned in 'ST0'.

7. Once the callee has finished processing, it restores 'ESP' from 'EBP' if it had allocated local stack space, then pops the previous value of 'EBP', and returns via 'RET' .

8. When the caller regains control from the callee, the function parameters are still on the stack, so it typically adds an immediate constant to 'ESP' to remove them (instead of executing a number of slow 'POP' instructions). Thus, if a function is accidentally called with the wrong number of parameters due to a prototype mismatch, the stack will still be returned to a sensible state since the caller, which _knows_ how many parameters it pushed, does the removing.

consider the Pascal code:

```
var zot:record  x,y:integer; z:double; end;
function foo( x,y:integer; z:double):integer;begin foo:=x+y end;
procedure bar;
var   x, y:integer;
         z:double ;
begin
     x:=foo(1,2,3.0);
end
```

The memory allocation, if nested functions did not exist in Pascal, could be implemented as shown in figure 5.1.

Note that the addresses of parameters and variables can be specified relative either to a special register called the frame pointer or to the stack pointer. If your code does not dynamically push things onto the stack or if your compiler keeps track of the stack position, then the SP register may be prefered. In Vector Pascal however, as is conventional with most other Pascal compilers we use the Frame Pointer register to access parameters and variables.

Key points:

1. If you address via the frame pointer (EBP on a Pentium) then the parameters have +ve addresses and the locals have -ve addresses.

2. If you address using the stack pointer they all have +ve addresses.

3. If you use the SP (ESP on a Pentium) the compiler has to take into account temporaries that are pushed on the stack.

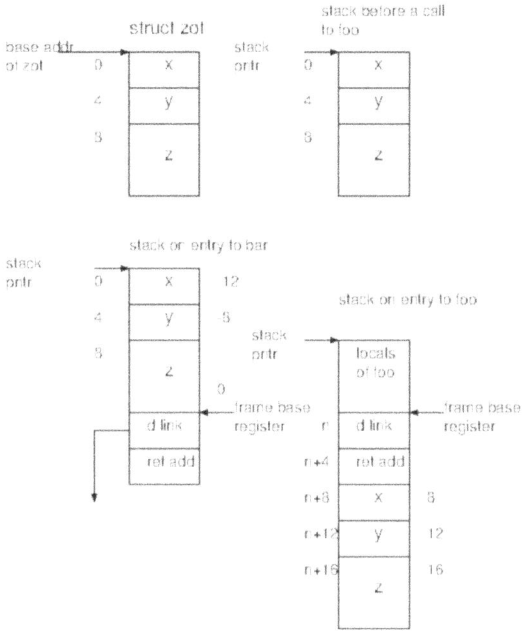

Figure 5.1: Stacks and records

5.3.3 Var Params

We have been assuming value parameters.

If we have var parameters (parameters which, when assigned to, change the value of the actual parameter) then the address of the parameter rather than the value of the parameter has to be passed on the stack. The compiler then places and extra level of indirection onto the addressing of the parameter.

5.3.4 Nested Functions

The existence of nesting of functions and procedures generates complexities that force us to use a more elaborate calling method than C. Consider the following Pascal example where we allow function nesting.

```
type vec1 = array[1..10] of  integer;
        scalar = integer;
function sum(var v:vec1);scalar;
  function total( i:scalar):scalar;
  begin
     total:=if i<1 then 0 else v[i]+total(i-1);
  end
  total(length(v))
```

Total recurses on i, but each invocation accesses the same copy of v.

Can we use the d-link to access v?

No

Consider the situation below

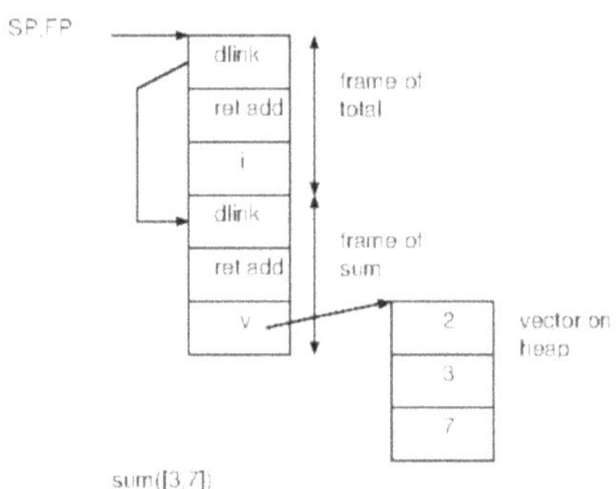

At this point we can access v at mem[dlink+8], but what happens on the next recursion?

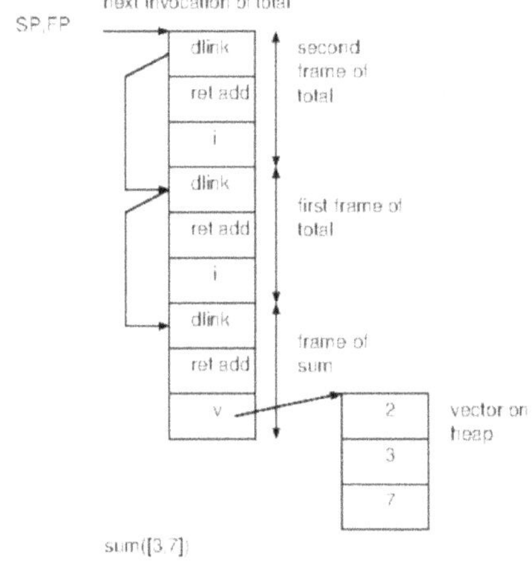

if we use mem[dlink+8] we get the previous version of i, v is now at mem[mem[dlink]+8] We need an alternative approach. There are 3 practical alternatives:

- Displays
- Static Links
- Lambda Lifting

We have chosen to use displays since Intel hardware provides support for these. They do place slight restrictions on function parameters[1], but it was felt that the simplicity of display implementation, and the ability to use the same calling mechanism as C outweighed this.

Displays

These can use the Intel Enter instruction defined as:

```
enter storage,level
 push ebp
```

[1]A functions f may not be an actual parameter to procedure or function g, if the scope of g outer to that of f

```
temp:=esp
if level>0
then
     repeat (level-1) times
       ebp:=ebp-4
       push dword[ebp]
     end repeat
     push temp
fi
ebp:=temp
esp:=esp - storage
```

For machines other than the Intel family, you, as a compiler modifier, have to generate sequences of simpler instructions to emulate the Intel Enter instruction.

Up to now we have assumed procedures use

```
enter xxx,0
```

Consider the effect of using enter 0,1 for sum and enter 0,2 for total :

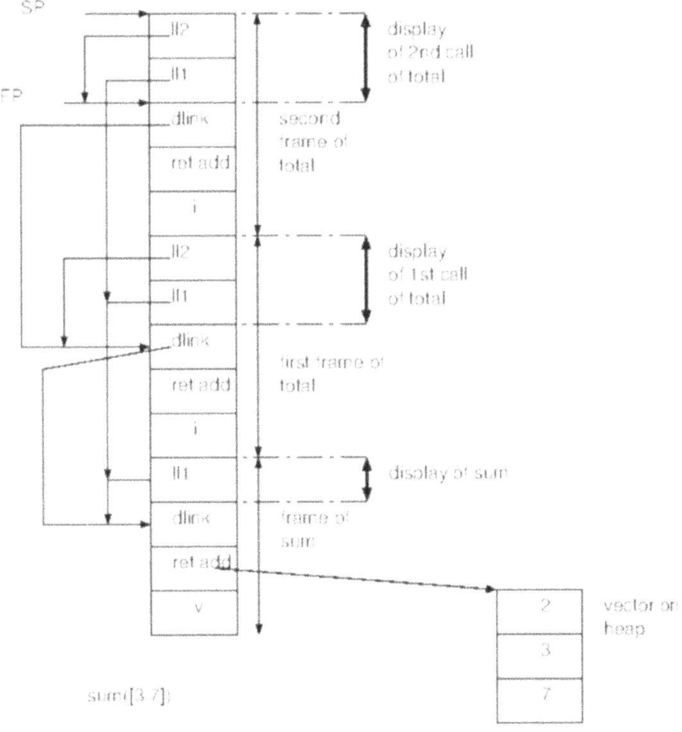

All variables are now addressed as a pair (lexlevel,offset), where an outer level function is lexical level 1, the first nested function is lexical level 2 etc.

A parameter can now be addressed as

```
mem[ display[lexlevel]+offset]
```

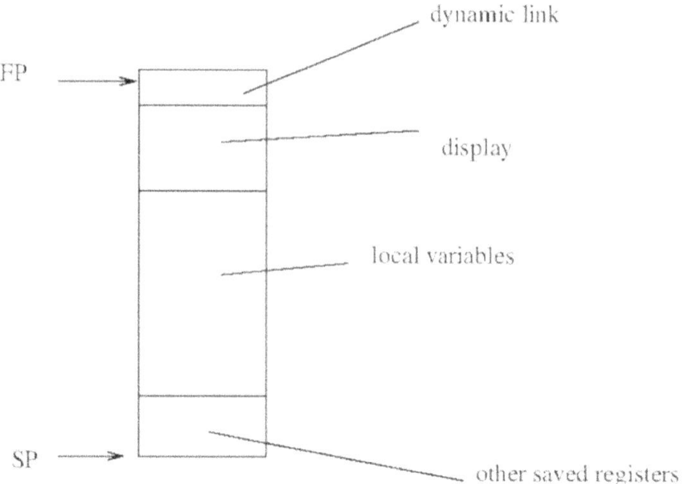

Figure 5.2: Full stack frame layout

The display is an array in memory at the start of the current frame. Using this notation, parameter i is always addressed as

```
mem[display[2]+8]= mem[ mem[fp-8]+8]
```

and v is always at

```
mem[display[1]+8]
```

hh

Optimisations FP always points to the current lexical level so at lexical level 2 we have

```
  mem[display[2]+8]
= mem[ mem[fp-8]+8]
= mem[fp+8]
```

Likewise we can chose to cache other display values in registers so avoiding repeated dereferencing of the display on stack.

Other registers sometimes have to be saved because of the definition of the ABI of the processor. If this is the case then they are saved after space has been reserved for local variables as shown in Figure 5.2.

5.3.5 Detail of calling method used on the Pentium

Procedure parameters are passed using a modified C calling convention to facilitate calls to external C procedures. Parameters are pushed on to the stack from right to left. Value parameters are pushed entire onto the stack, var parameters are pushed as addresses.

Example

```
program callconv;
type t1= record a,b:integer end;
var
   x,y:t1;
  procedure foo(var a:t1; b:t1; c:integer);
  begin
  end;

  function bar:t1;
  begin bar:=y;end;

begin
        x:=bar;
        foo(x,y,3);
end.
```

This would generate the following code for the procedure foo.

```
; procedure generated by code generator class ilcg.tree.PentiumCG;0
label114b8f429f3a:;0
;  foo;0
; entering a procedure at lexical level 1;0
 enter spaceforfoo11-4*1,1;   create display and variable space
push ebx;              save registers as demanded by Linux ABI
push esi;
push edi;
; ------------------          Code for Foo would go here if
;-------------------          it were not a null procedure

spaceforfoo11 equ 4;          declare space needed this is done here
                  ;          because the code generation may cause
                  ;          new temporary vars to be needed so
                  ;          we dont know the space required to here
foo11exit:;2
pop edi;               restore saved registers
pop esi;0
pop ebx;0
leave;                        restore old stack frame
 ret 0;                       pop return address into PC
```

and the calling code is

```
 push DWORD      3;                     right most parameter 3
 lea esp,[  esp+     -8];               create space for y on stack
 movq MM4, [   PmainBase+     -16];     fetch y
 movq  [ esp],MM4;                      store on the stack
```

```
push DWORD   PmainBase+     -8;        push the address of x
EMMS ;                                 clear mmx status flags
 call label114b8f429f3a;               call the procedure
add esp, 16;                           restore the stack
```

Function results

Function results are returned in registers for scalars following the C calling convention for the operating system on which the compiler is implemented. Records, strings and sets are returned by the caller passing an implicit parameter containing the address of a temporary buffer in the calling environment into which the result can be assigned. Given the following program

The call of `bar` in the previous example would generate

```
push DWORD   PmainBase+     -24;        pass the address of a result buffer
call label114b8f429f712;                call the function
add esp, 4;                             restore the stack
movq MM4, [   PmainBase+     -24];      get the result buffer in MM4
movq  [   PmainBase+     -8],MM4;       store in x
```

5.4 Multi-core Parallelism

SIMD vectorisation works for one dimensional data, or on the last dimension for arrays stored in row major order, because the hardware has to work on adjacent words. SIMD gives considerable acceleration on image data, and worthwhile accelerations on floating point and integer data. Future machines like the Larrabee will have considerably wider SIMD registers, increasing the benefits of SIMD code. But newer chips also have multiple cores. For these, the recent versions of the Vector Pascal compiler will parallelise across multiple cores if the arrays being worked on are of rank 2. The Pascal source code of the program remains the same independently of whether it is being targeted at a simple sequential machine, a SIMD machine or a multi-core SIMD machine. Targeting is done by flags passed to the compiler:

```
vpc sub2dex -cpu486
```

would compile sub2dex.pas using purely sequential 32 bit instructions.

```
vpc sub2dex -cpuOpteron
```

would compile the same file targeted to a 64 bit Opteron with 1 core using the SIMD instructions in the Opteron instructionset.

```
vpc sub2dex -cpuOpteron -cores2
```

Algorithm 5.1 Example of combined mult-core and SIMD parallelism.

```
procedure sub2d;
type range=0..127;
var x,y,z:array[range,range] of real;
begin
        x:=y-z;
end;
```

This translates into ILCG as follows when compiled for a dual core Opteron

```
procedure(sub2d,
 procedure (label12                    )
 post_job[label12,^(%rbp),1];   /*              */
 /* Note that %rbp is the Opteron stack frame pointer */
 post_job[label12,^(%rbp),0];   /*              */
 wait_on_done[0];
 wait_on_done[1];
)
```

would compile the file to a 64 bit Opteron with 2 cores and SIMD instructions. The compiler is implemented in Java so the selection of code generators and compilation strategies is achieved by dynamically loading appropriate compiler and code generator classes.

Let us now look at the transformations required to achieve this using a trivial rank 2 array example in Algorithm 5.1. The example is not intended to be realistic or useful, only illustrative. We assume that the code has been compiled for a dual core Opteron.

Two threads are dispatched to process the work using a fork - rejoin paradigm. The run time library is built on top of pthreads. For a two core machine, two server threads are initiated at program start up. These wait on a semaphore until post_job passes them the address of a procedure and a stack frame context within which the procedure is to be executed.

The statement x:=y-z is translated into a procedure that can run as a separate task, the ILCG has been simplified for comprehensibility in Algorithm 5.2.

The basic structure of the task procedure is two nested for loops, one for each dimension of the arrays.

The outer loop or row index steps by 2 to ensure that each task will process every 2nd row, starting at the row given by the task number. Thus task 0 will process rows 0,2,4,6,... Task 1 will proocess rows 1,3,5,7,... If there are 4 cores available each task will process every 4th row, etc.

The inner loop, for the column indices, advances by 4 since the Opteron has SIMD registers capable of handling 4 floating point numbers at a time.

5.4.1 The PURE Function Extension

We define a pure function to be such that does not have any side effects, i.e. it does not update any global, or shared, states outside of its own scope. If

Algorithm 5.2 The function performing nested loops.

```
procedure (label12 /*                    */ ,
 for(mem(+(^(%rbp),-24)),^(mem(+(^(%rbp),16))),127  ,   2,
    /*                                                      */
  var(mem(+(^(%rbp),-32))),/* iota[1] */
  for(mem(+(^(%rbp),-32)), 0    ,127,     4 ,
    /*                                   */
   mem(ref ieee32 vector ( 4 ), /*                     */
       +(+(*(^(mem(+(^(%rbp),-24))),512),
         +(*(^(mem(+(^(%rbp),-32))),  4),-131072)),
           ^(mem(+(^(%rbp),-8))))):=
     -(^(mem(ref ieee32 vector ( 4 ),/*                      */
       +(+(*(^(mem(+(^(%rbp),-24))),512),
         +(*(^(mem(+(^(%rbp),-32))),  4),-196608)),
           ^(mem(+(^(%rbp),-8)))))),
       ^(mem(ref ieee32 vector ( 4 ),/*                      */
         +(+(*(^(mem(+(^(%rbp), -24))),512),
           +(*(^(mem(+(^(%rbp), -32))),  4),-262144)),
             ^(mem(+(^(%rbp),-8))))))))),

 )
```

the other functions are called from the body of the function, these also have to be pure even if not marked as such. This definition of pure functions is consistent with the definition used in FORTRAN 95. Given the absence of explicit multi-threading constructs in the given language, the above property of pure functions implies thread safety. A function can be labeled as pure by prepending the keyword `pure` in front of every declaration or definition of the function. This means that if, for example, a function is declared as pure in the interface section of the programme, it must be also declared as pure anywhere else in the code, e.g. in the subsequent definition of the function body. Any inconsistency in the declared purity of a function is spotted by the compiler and treated as a syntactic error.

```
pure function next(i : integer): integer;
begin
        next := i+1;
end;
```

Above function *next* operates only on the parameter passed to it, thus it is appropriate to declare it as pure. The keyword *pure* does not bare any semantic value, other than it serves as a hint to the compiler which may then generate multi-threaded code. Multi-threaded code will be generated if -cores$n$ flag is passed to the compiler specifying more than one core, and hence the number of threads, available to the programme and if the function is then invoked as part of an assignment statement.

5.4.2 Task Parallelism and Block Structure

The technique of procedurising code shown in Algorithms 5.1 and 5.2 is well established when parallelising loops in Open-MP. There are two significant differences. First, and least significantly, in Vector Pascal the loop is implicit rather

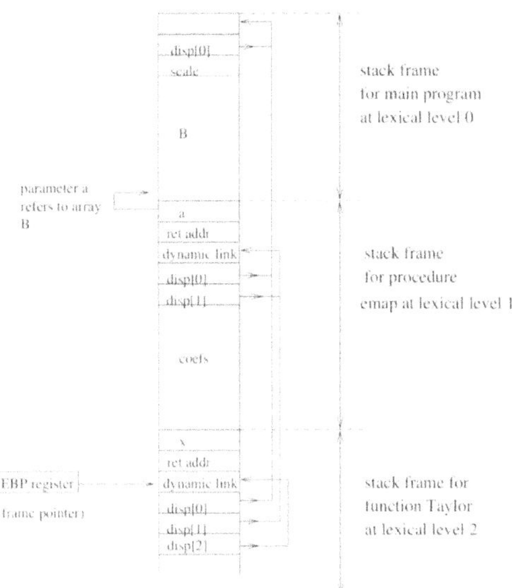

Figure 5.3: Stack for nestpar in single core mode.

than the explicit loops used in Open-MP. But secondly Open-MP is targeted at C and FORTRAN which are flat languages. Pascal is a block structured language which makes the access to variables by spawned tasks somewhat more complex. Consider Algorithm 5.4.2 which illustrates the use of nested blocks in Pascal. This has a main program `nestpar` and embedded within that a procedure `emap` which takes a matrix a as a parameter and replaces each $a_{i,j}$ with $e^{scale.a_{i,j}}$ where *scale* is a global variable. The exponential function is approximated by a Taylor series

$$e^x = 1 + \frac{1}{1!}x^1 + \frac{1}{1!}x^1 + \frac{1}{2!}x^2 + \frac{1}{3!}x^3 + ...$$

using the function `Taylor`. The Taylor series is evaluated as
$Taylor \leftarrow \sum (coefs \times x^{\iota_0})$;
where $\iota_0 = 0, 1, 2, 3...$ using the line

```
Taylor:=   \+ (coefs * x pow iota[0]);
```

The coefs vector has been initialised in the main program to contain the inverse factorial series as required.

There are a number of references from inner to outer scopes: `Taylor` uses the vector `coefs`, and `emap` uses the variable `scale`. There are three well known techniques for implementing this in normal procedural code: λlifting, static chaining or display vectors. Since Intel provide direct hardware support for display vectors in the procedure ENTER and LEAVE instructions we have chosen to use displays. Figure 5.3 illustrates how the stack would be organised during execution of Taylor when the program is compiled for a single core machine. Observe how Taylor can access variables in the enclosing stack frames using the display vector. But if the code is to run on a dual core machine there will be not one but three stacks as shown in Figure 5.4: one for the main program and

Algorithm 5.3 Taylor series example.

```
program nestpar;
type t = array[1..3,1..2] of real;
     coef=array[0..5] of real;
                { tabulate inverse factorials }
const expc:coef=(1,1,1/2,1/6,1/24,1/(5*24));
var scale:real;B:t;
procedure emap(var a:t);
  { for each a[i,j] replace with a[i,j]+exp(scale*a[i,j]) }
  var coefs:coef;
  pure function Taylor( x:real):real;
  begin
    Taylor:=  \+ (coefs * x pow iota[0]);
  end;
begin
   coefs:= expc;
   a := Taylor(a*scale);
end;
begin
     scale:=0.1;
     B:= iota[0]*iota[1];
     write(B);
     emap(B);
     write(B);
end.
```

Output Produced

```
1.00000    2.00000
2.00000    4.00000
3.00000    6.00000

1.10517    1.22140
1.22140    1.49182
1.34986    1.82205
```

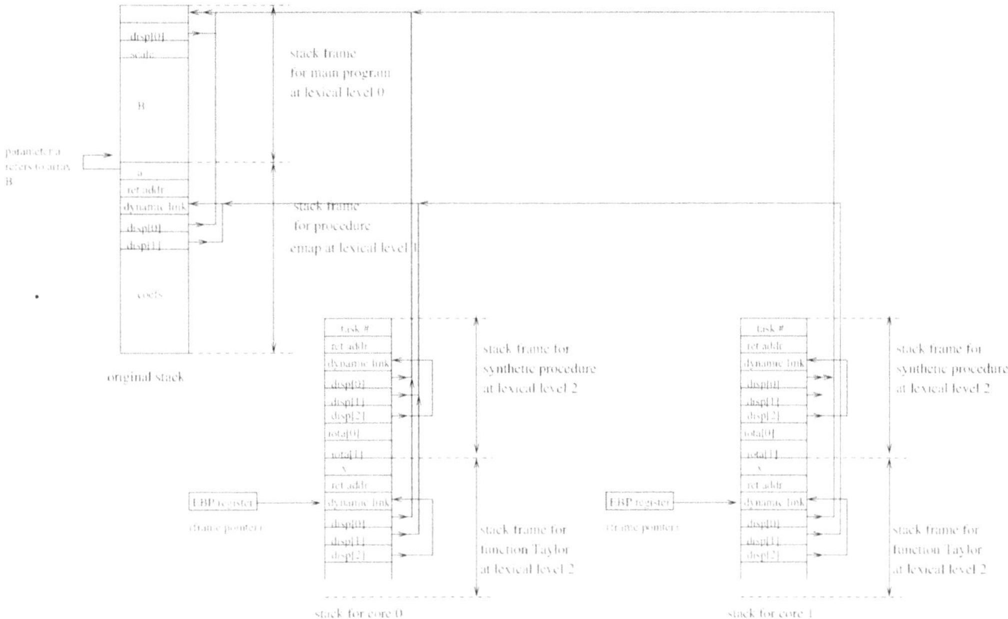

Figure 5.4: The 3 stacks used by nestpar in dual core mode.

one each for the child tasks. The original function `emap` will have been written to ILCG equivalent to:

```
procedure emap(var a:t);
  var coefs:coef;
  pure function Taylor( x:real):real;
  begin
    Taylor:=    \+ (coefs * x pow iota[0]);
  end;
  procedure dummy(start:int);
  var iota:array[0..1] of integer;
  begin
    iota[0]:=start;
    while iota[0]<=3 do
    begin
      for iota[1]:=1 to 2 do
       a[iota[0],iota[1]]:=Taylor(a[iota[0],iota[1]]*scale);
      iota[0]:=iota[0]+2;
    end;
  end;
begin
   coefs:= expc;
   post_job(dummy,1);post_job(dummy,0);
   wait_on_done(0);wait_on_done(1);
end;
```

The function `dummy` has to run on a task stack and yet have access to the variable `a` in `emap` and `scale` in the main program, both of which are executing on the main stack. It then has to call `Taylor` in such a way as to ensure that `Taylor` can access the global `scale`. Provided that the displays can be set up as shown in Figure 5.4, this will work, but it is impossible to set up the displays this way when using standard intel call conventions along with the `pthreads` library. Whenever a function is executed within a thread it is allocated a new stack that does not contain display pointers, hence variables from containing scopes cannot be accessed.

In order to support sharing of the global stack amongst multiple tasks, we have implemented an assembly routine *taskexecute*, which corresponds to the following C function signature:

```
void taskexecute(struct threadblock *);
```

As can be seen, the function expects a single parameter which is a pointer to a structure of type *struct threadblock* defined as

```
struct threadblock{
    char * savedframepointer;
    char * savedcodepointer;
    int threadnumber;
}
```

Above, `savedframerpointer` is the pointer to the original stack in which the displays are already setup, `savedcodepointer` is the pointer to the function that is being parallelised, and `threadnumber` is a number in the range$0..n-1$ for a programme running on$n$ cores.. The following assembly code implements `taskexecute` on the Pentium architecture.

Assembly code sequence required to implement the task execute

```
.globl taskexecute
taskexecute:
# on entry we have a pointer in %esp to the task block
# this task block has the C definition
# struct threadblock{
#         char * savedframepointer;
#         char * savedcodepointer;
#         int threadnumber;}
# the first thing we do is save the framepointer on entry
push %ebp
# next get the address of the stored frame pointer in the task block
mov 8(%esp) , %eax
#we load the frame pointer into the hardware frame pointer (ebp)
mov 0(%eax), %ebp
# get the task number
push 8(%eax)
# make the call on the task
call * 4(%eax)
# unwind stack pointer
add $4,%esp
# restore framepointer we were called with
pop %ebp
ret
```

The essence of this form of implementation is that the pthread is setup to execute `taskexecute` which is passed `threadblock` from the calling environment that contains the stack pointer used by the calling environment. `taskexecute` substitutes the stack allocated by the pthread library with the above stack before executing the code sequence contained in the `savedcodepointer`. The effect of substituting the stack pointer is undone once the called code sequence halts to ensure a clean exit of the wrapper.

5.5 Example Programs

5.5.1 Image convolution

The first example we will look at is the use of a seperable convolution kernel to blur an image. Convolution of an image by a matrix of real numbers can be used to smooth or sharpen an image, depending on the matrix used. If A is an output image, K a convolution matrix, then if B is the convolved image

$$B_{y,x} = \sum_i \sum_j A_{y+i,x+j} K_{i,j}$$

A separable convolution kernel is a vector of real numbers that can be applied independently to the rows and columns of an image to provide filtering. It is a specialisation of the more general convolution matrix, but is algorithmically more efficient to implement. We can do a seperable convolution provided that the kernel is formed by the outer product of two vectors **a**,**b**. A symmetric separable convolution can be done if $\mathbf{a} = \mathbf{b}$.

If $\mathbf{k}$ is a symmetric separable convolution vector, then the corresponding matrix K is such that $K_{i,j} = \mathbf{k}_i \mathbf{k}_j$.

Given a starting image A as a two dimensional array of pixels, and a three element kernel c_1, c_2, c_3, the algorithm first forms a temporary array T whose whose elements are the weighted sum of adjacent rows $T_{y,x} = c_1 A_{y-1,x} + c_2 A_{y,x} + c_3 A_{y+1,x}$. Then in a second phase it sets the original image to be the weighted sum of the columns of the temporary array: $A_{y,x} = c_1 T_{y,x-1} + c_2 T_{y,x} + c_3 Ty, x + 1$.

Clearly the outer edges of the image are a special case, since the convolution is defined over the neighbours of the pixel, and the pixels along the boundaries a missing one neighbour. A number of solutions are available for this, but for simplicity we will perform only vertical convolutions on the left and right edges and horizontal convolutions on the top and bottom lines of the image. A Vector Pascal routine to do this is given below. The source has been pretty printed in the latex format that is automatically generated by the compiler is listing enabled. An equivalent sequential C routine is given in Algorithm 5.4.

In comparing the C and Vector Pascal, note two features which give performance advantages to the Vector Pascal form of the algorithm.

1. The support for fixed point 8 bit arithmetic with the pixel type. This allows a higher level of parallelism to be achieved since a P4 or AMD64 can in principle operate on 16 $\times$8 bit numbers with a single instruction. Lacking these types, the C algorithm has to use 32 bit floats. The pixel type automatically uses saturated arithmetic.

2. The data parallel form of expression of the Vector Pascal allows more efficient optimisation of the code.

Vector Pascal convolution algorithm

```
type
   plane(rows,cols:integer )= array [0..rows ,0..cols ] of pixel ;
var
   Let T, I ∈^plane;
   Let i ∈ integer;
   begin
```

Allocates a temporary buffer to hold a plane, and 3 temporary buffers to hold the convolution co-ordinates as lines of pixels.

```
   new ( T ,im .maxrow ,im .maxcol );
   new ( I ,3,im .maxcol );
   I↑[0]← c1;
   I↑[1]← c2;
   I↑[2]← c3;
```

Perform convolution on each of the planes of the image. This has to be done with an explicit loop as array maps only works with functions not with procedures.

```
   for i← 0 to im.maxplane do convpar (im_i, I↑, T↑); { see section 5.5.1}
```

This sequence frees the temporary buffers used in the convolution process.

```
   dispose ( I );
   dispose ( T );
end ;
```

convpar

```
procedure convpar ( var p ,I ,T :plane );
```

This convolves a plane by applying the vertical and horizontal convolutions in turn.

var
  Let r, $c \in$ integer;
begin

This sequence performs a vertical convolution of the rows of the plane p and places the result in the temporary plane T. It uses the lines of pixels l[i] as convolution weights. Use of lines of pixels rather than the floating point numbers for the kernel weights allows the computation to proceed 8 pixels at a time in parallel. The lines $T_0 \leftarrow p_0$; and $T_r \leftarrow p_r$; deal with the top and bottom rows of the picture which are left unchanged.

`{$r-}{disable range checks}`
$r \leftarrow p.rows$;
$T_{1..r-1} \leftarrow p_{0..r-2} \times l_0 + p_{1..r-1} \times l_1 + p_{2..r} \times l_2$;
$T_0 \leftarrow p_0$;
$T_r \leftarrow p_r$;

Now perform a horizontal convolution of the plane T and place the result in p.

$c \leftarrow p.cols$;
$p_{0..r,1..c-1} \leftarrow T_{0..r,0..c-2} \times l_0 + T_{0..r,2..c} \times l_2 + T_{0..r,1..c-1} \times l_1$;
$p_{0..r,0} \leftarrow T_{0..r,0}$;
$p_{0..r,c} \leftarrow T_{0..r,c}$;
`{$r+}{enable range checks}`

end ;

5.6 Array representation

The maximum number of array dimensions supported in the compiler is 5.

A static array is represented simply by the number of bytes required to store the array being allocated in the global segment or on the stack.

A dynamic array is always represented on the heap. Since its rank is known to the compiler what needs to be stored at run time are the bounds and the means to access it. For simplicity we make the format of dynamic and conformant arrays the same. Thus for schema

```
s(a,b,c,d:integer)= array[a..b,c..d] of integer
```

whose run time bounds are evaluated to be 2..4,3..7 we would have the following structure:

Algorithm 5.4 C version of the convolution routine.

```
#include <stdlib.h>
conv(char *im, int planes, int rows,int cols,float c1,float c2,float c3)
/* C version of a convolution routine */
{
 int i,j,p,temp;
 int planestep=rows*cols;
 char * plane, * buffplane;
 char * buff = malloc( rows*planes*cols);
 for (p=0;p<planes;p++){
  plane = &im[p*planestep];
  buffplane= &buff[p*planestep];
  /* convolve horizontally */
  for(i=0;i<rows;i++){
   for(j=1;j<(cols-1);j++) {
    temp= plane[i*cols+j-1]*c1+plane[i*cols+j]*c2+plane[i*cols+j+1]*c3;
    if (temp<0){temp=0;}
    else if (temp>255) { temp=255;} ;
    buffplane[i*cols+j]=temp;
   }
   buffplane[i*cols]=plane[i*cols];
   buffplane[i*cols+cols-1]=plane[i*cols+cols-1];
  }
/* convolve vertically */
  for(j=0;j<cols;j++) {
   for(i=1;i<rows-1;i++){
    temp= buffplane[(i-1)*cols+j]*c1+buffplane[i*cols+j]*c2+buffplane[(1+i)*
    if(temp<0){temp=0;}
    else if (temp>255) { temp=255;} ;
    plane[i*cols+j]=temp;
   }
   plane[j]=buffplane[j];
   plane[(rows-1)*cols+j]=buffplane[ (rows-1)*cols+j];
  }
 }
 free(buff);
}
```

address	field	value
x	base of data	address of first integer in the array
x+4	a	2
x+8	b	4
x+12	step	20
x+16	c	3
x+20	d	7

The base address for a schematic array on the heap, will point at the first byte after the array header show. For a conformant array, it will point at the first data byte of the array or array range being passed as a parameter. The step field specifies the length of an element of the second dimension in bytes. It is included to allow for the case where we have a conformant array formal parameter

`x:array[a..b:integer,c..d:integer] of integer`

to which we pass as actual parameter the range

`p[2..4,3..7]`

as actual parameter, where `p:array[1..10,1..10] of integer`

In this case the base address would point at @p[2,3] and the step would be 40 - the length of 10 integers.

5.6.1 Range checking

When arrays are indexed, the compiler plants run time checks to see if the indices are within bounds. In many cases the optimiser is able to remove these checks, but in those cases where it is unable to do so, some performance degradation can occur. Range checks can be disabled or enabled by the compiler directives.

{$r-} { disable range checks }

{$r+} { enable range checks }

Performance can be further enhanced by the practice of declaring arrays to have lower bounds of zero. The optimiser is generally able to generate more efficient code for zero based arrays.

Index

Bibliography

[1] 3L Limited, Parallel C V2.2, Software Product Description, 1995.

[2] Advanced Micro Devices, 3DNow! Technology Manual, 1999.

[3] Aho, A.V., Ganapathi, M, TJiang S.W.K., Code Generation Using Tree Matching and Dynamic Programming, ACM Trans, Programming Languages and Systems 11, no.4, 1989, pp.491-516.

[4] Blelloch, G. E., NESL: A Nested Data-Parallel Language, Carnegie Mellon University, CMU-CS-95-170, Sept 1995.

[5] Burke, Chris, J User Manual, ISI, 1995.

[6] Cattell R. G. G., Automatic derivation of code generators from machine descriptions, ACM Transactions on Programming Languages and Systems, 2(2), pp. 173-190, April 1980.

[7] Chaitin. G., Elegant Lisp Programs, in The Limits of Mathematics, pp. 29-56, Springer, 1997.

[8] Cheong, G., and Lam, M., An Optimizer for Multimedia Instruction Sets, 2nd SUIF Workshop, Stanford University, August 1997.

[9] Cherry, G., W., Pascal Programming Structures, Reston Publishing, Reston, 1980.

[10] Cockshott, Paul, Direct Compilation of High Level Languages for Multimedia Instruction-sets, Department of Computer Science, University of Glasgow, Nov 2000.

[11] Ewing, A. K., Richardson, H., Simpson, A. D., Kulkarni, R., Writing Data Parallel Programs with High Performance Fortran, Edinburgh Parallel Computing Centre, Ver 1.3.1.

[12] Formella, A.; Obe, A.; Paul, W.; Rauber, T. & Schmidt, D. The SPARK 2.0 system-a special purpose vector processor with a VectorPASCAL compiler System Sciences, 1992. Proceedings of the Twenty-Fifth Hawaii International Conference on, 1992, 1, 547-558.

[13] Susan L. Graham, Table Driven Code Generation, IEEE Computer, Vol 13, No. 8, August 1980, pp 25..37.

[14] Intel, Intel Architecture Software Developers Manual Volumes 1 and 2, 1999.

[15] Intel, Willamette Processor Software Developer's Guide, February, 2000.

[16] ISO, Extended Pascal ISO 10206:1990, 1991.

[17] ISO, Pascal, ISO 7185:1990, 1991.

[18] K. E. Iverson, A Programming Language, John Wiley & Sons, Inc., New York (1962), p. 16.

[19] Iverson, K. E. . Notation as a tool of thought. Communications of the ACM, 23(8), 444-465, 1980.

[20] Iverson K. E, A personal View of APL, IBM Systems Journal, Vol 30, No 4, 1991.

[21] Iverson, Kenneth E., J Introduction and Dictionary, Iverson Software Inc. (ISI), Toronto, Ontario, 1995. 4, pp 347-361, 2000.

[22] Jensen, K., Wirth, N., PASCAL User Manual and Report, Springer 1978.

[23] Johnston, D., C++ Parallel Systems, ECH: Engineering Computing Newsletter, No. 55, Daresbury Laboratory/Rutherford Appleton Laboratory, March 1995,pp 6-7.

[24] Knuth, D., Computers and Typesetting, Addison Wesley, 1994.

[25] Krall, A., and Lelait, S., Compilation Techniques for Multimedia Processors, International Journal of Parallel Programming, Vol. 28, No. 4, pp 347-361, 2000.

[26] Lamport, L., LaTeXa document preparation system, Addison Wesley, 1994.

[27] Leupers, R., Compiler Optimization for Media Processors, EMMSEC 99/Sweden 1999.

[28] Metcalf, M., and Reid., J., The F Programming Language, OUP, 1996.

[29] Peleg, A., Wilke S., Weiser U., Intel MMX for Multimedia PCs, Comm. ACM, vol 40, no. 1 1997.

[30] Shannon, C., A Mathematical Theory of Communication, The Bell System Technical Journal, Vol 27, pp 379-423 and 623-656, 1948.

[31] Snyder, L., A Programmer's Guide to ZPL, MIT Press, Cambridge, Mass, 1999.

[32] Srereman, N., and Govindarajan, G., A Vectorizing Compiler for Multimedia Extensions, International Journal of Parallel Programming, Vol. 28, No. 4, pp 363-400, 2000.

[33] Strachey, C., Fundamental Concepts of Programming Languages, University of Oxford, 1967.

[34] Étienne Gagnon, SABLECC, AN OBJECT-ORIENTED COMPILER FRAMEWORK, School of Computer Science McGill University, Montreal, March 1998.

[35] Texas Instruments, TMS320C62xx CPU and Instruction Set Reference Guide, 1998.

[36] Turner, T. Vector Pascal: a computer programming language for the FPS-164 array processor Iowa State Univ. of Science and Technology, Ames (USA), 1.

[37] Wirth, N., Recollections about the development of Pascal, in *History of Programming Languages-II*, ACM-Press, pp 97-111, 1996.

www.ingramcontent.com/pod-product-compliance
Lightning Source LLC
Chambersburg PA
CBHW081053170526
45165CB00006B/2266

* 9 7 8 1 4 4 7 7 6 1 5 6 3 *